DK CHILDREN'S EVERYDAY BIBLE

Illustrated by
ANNA C LEPLAR

Stories retold by
DEBORAH
CHANCELLOR

LONDON, NEW YORK, MUNICH,
MELBOURNE, AND DELHI

Project Editor Jane Chapman
Art Editors Jane Horne and Peter Bailey
Managing Editor Linda Esposito
Managing Art Editor Diane Thistlethwaite
US Editor Gary Werner
DTP Designer Louise Paddick
Jacket Design Victoria Harvey
Production Shivani Pandey
Indexer Lynn Bresler
Religious consultant Penny Boshoff

First American Edition, 2002

10 9 8 7

Published in the United States by
DK Publishing, Inc.
375 Hudson Street
New York, NY 10014

A catalog record for this book is available from the Library of Congress.
ISBN 0-7894-8858-2   ISBN 978-0-7894-8858-9

Color reproduction by Colourscan, Singapore
Printed and bound in Singapore by Tien Wah Press

see our complete product line at
www.dk.com

INTRODUCTION

The *Children's Everyday Bible* takes children on a wonderful journey through the Bible from beginning to end. With a new story for each day of the year, this unique collection brings the people, places, and key events of the Bible vividly to life.

In the Old Testament stories, God speaks through the lives of different men and women. The adventures of Moses, Daniel, Jonah, and many others will inspire children to think about different emotions, such as love, happiness, hatred, and fear. The stories of the New Testament tell about the life of Jesus, the long-awaited Messiah. Children will hear about the miracles that he performed and see how Jesus' work continued after his death.

Beginning on January 1, the stories follow the order that they appear in the Bible. But, as each story stands on its own, children can choose to read through a day at a time or dip into stories at random. Younger children in particular will love to flick through the book, looking at the pictures and selecting a story to be read to them. They will enjoy going back to their favorite stories again and again and looking up dates that are special to them, such as birthdays. With older children, you may want to ask follow-up questions about the stories they have read to test their understanding.

The *Everyday Bible* is like a treasure chest that can be opened and enjoyed by the whole family – every day of the year.

CONTENTS

CONTENTS

NEW TESTAMENT

CONTENTS

BIBLE LANDS

Rome

Puteoli

ITALY

BULGARIA

Philippi

Berea

Thessalonica

PAUL AND
SILAS
IMPRISONED

Troas

GREECE

SICILY

Athens

Corinth

Ephesus

PAUL
SHIPWRECKED

MALTA

CRETE

Mediterranean Sea

THE HOLY
LAND

Zarephath

JESUS FEEDS
THE CROWD

Capernaum

Cana

Nazareth

Shunem

*Sea of
Galilee*

Caesarea

MOSES IN THE
BULRUSHES

Samaria

Joppa

Shiloh

EGYPT

Lydda

Gibeon

Jericho

N

Emmaus

Jerusalem

Bethany

Bethlehem

W

E

THE BIRTH
OF JESUS

S

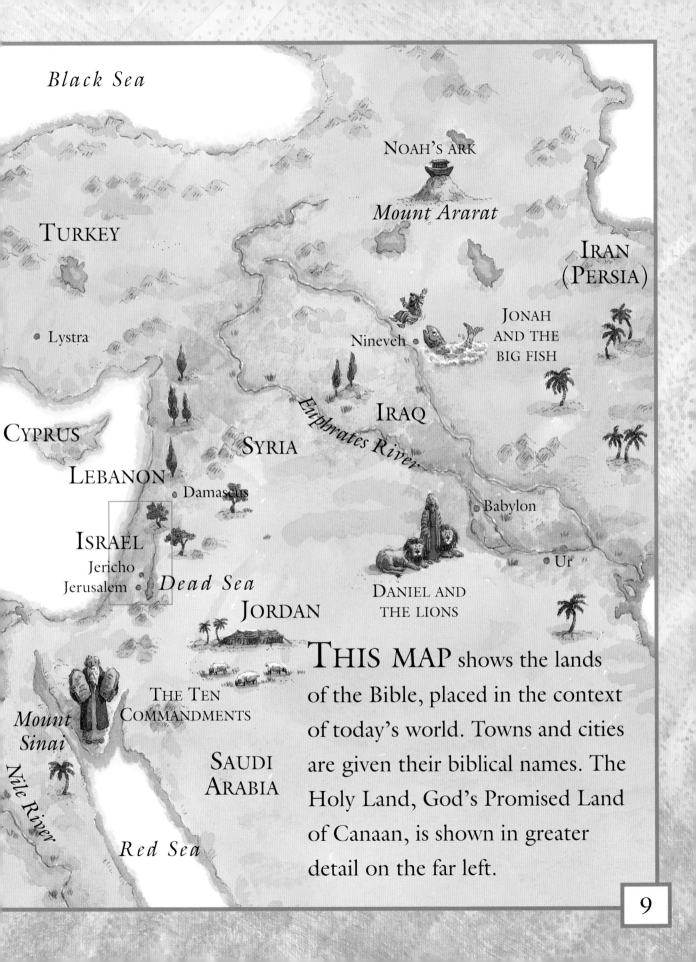

Black Sea

TURKEY

NOAH'S ARK

Mount Ararat

IRAN (PERSIA)

Lystra

Nineveh

JONAH AND THE BIG FISH

CYPRUS

Euphrates River

IRAQ

SYRIA

LEBANON

Damascus

Babylon

ISRAEL

Jericho

Jerusalem

Dead Sea

DANIEL AND THE LIONS

Ur

JORDAN

THE TEN COMMANDMENTS

Mount Sinai

SAUDI ARABIA

Nile River

Red Sea

THIS MAP shows the lands of the Bible, placed in the context of today's world. Towns and cities are given their biblical names. The Holy Land, God's Promised Land of Canaan, is shown in greater detail on the far left.

9

JANUARY 1

IN THE BEGINNING, God made the world. At first, the Earth was covered with a vast, dark ocean. So God commanded light to break up the gloom. Then God began to bring order to his world. He told the waters to move back, and dry land appeared, which separated the seas. The land was empty, so God filled it with all kinds of plants and trees. Pretty flowers brought color to God's new creation. Next God turned to the skies. He ordered the sun to shine by day and the moon by night. Then he made stars that twinkled in the night like bright lights.

JANUARY 2

GOD WAS VERY PLEASED with the
world he had created. But his work was not
finished. The sky and the sea were quiet.
So God made living creatures, who could
fly in the air and swim in the water. Soon the
heavens and oceans were teeming with life.
Then God turned his attention to the land, which was
beautiful but empty. So God created all the animals,
from the smallest mite to the biggest beast, and
they roamed throughout the Earth.

JANUARY 3

THERE WAS SOMETHING MISSING

from God's new world. The most wonderful part was still to come. God made human beings with minds to think and hearts to love. The first man was called Adam. God realized that Adam was lonely, so he made Eve, the first woman. Adam and Eve lived together in a perfect place called the Garden of Eden. God was pleased with his creation.

JANUARY 4

ADAM AND EVE were very happy in the Garden of Eden. They were friends with God, their maker, and they enjoyed everything that he had created. They were in charge of God's world, but in return God wanted them to obey him. He loved them and knew what was best for them. There were many trees laden with tasty fruit in the Garden of Eden, but there was just one tree that God did not want Adam and Eve to touch. This was the Tree of Knowledge of Good and Evil. "If you eat the fruit of that tree, you will die," said God.

JANUARY 5

EVE WAS WALKING in the Garden of Eden when she came across a snake, the craftiest of all God's animals. The snake told Eve about the tree that God had told them not to touch. "If you eat the fruit from this tree," said the snake, "you will be like God, because you will know what is good and what is bad." Eve was tempted to disobey God, so she took a bite of the forbidden fruit. Then she persuaded Adam to do the same. When God found out what they had done, he was angry and sad. He told Adam and Eve to leave the Garden of Eden forever.

JANUARY 6

ADAM AND EVE had two sons, named Cain and Abel. Cain was a farmer, and Abel was a shepherd. One day, the brothers offered presents to God. Cain brought some ripe corn, and Abel offered a lamb.

God looked into the hearts of the men, not just at their gifts. He knew Abel loved him, so he accepted his offering. But he knew Cain was selfish, so he refused his gift. Cain was furious with God and jealous of his brother. When they were alone together, Cain killed Abel. To punish Cain, God sent him away from home to live a sad and lonely life.

JANUARY 7

GOD WAS NO LONGER HAPPY with the world he had created. The people had turned away from him and were living wicked lives. God decided to send a flood to wash away everything that was bad. But there was one old man, Noah, who still loved and obeyed God. So God asked Noah to build a big wooden ark. He gave him special instructions to follow. Then God told him to gather together two of every kind of living creature on Earth, one male and one female.

JANUARY 8

NOAH DID EVERYTHING that he was asked to do: he built the ark, gathered all the animals, and stowed away enough food for them to eat. Then, two by two, the animals climbed into the ark – it was a tight fit! Finally, Noah got on board with his wife, his three sons, and their wives. God promised to keep them all safe.

JANUARY 9

THE HEAVENS OPENED and it began to pour with rain. Noah, his family, and all the animals were safe in the ark. It rained for forty days and forty nights, and floodwaters rose and covered the whole Earth. But then the rain stopped. The ark came aground on a mountain top. Noah sent out a dove, which flew back with an olive leaf in its beak. This was a sign that the Earth was no longer flooded. Then God told Noah it was time to leave the ark.

JANUARY 10

THE DOORS OF THE ARK were opened. The animals left to begin a new life and fill the Earth again. Noah and his family were very happy to be back on dry land, too. They gave thanks to God for keeping them safe. God promised that he would never again send such a terrible flood. As a sign and reminder of this promise, he placed a beautiful rainbow in the sky.

JANUARY 11

ABRAHAM LIVED in a comfortable house in the city of Ur. One day, God said something very surprising to Abraham. "Leave this city and go to a land that I will show to you. If you do this, I will bless you and make you great." Abraham was seventy-five years old, and it would not be easy for him to begin a traveler's life at this age. But he obeyed God and packed up all his belongings. He left home with his wife Sarah and his nephew Lot. They set off together, not sure of where they were going or how long their journey would take them.

JANUARY 12

ABRAHAM AND LOT owned many sheep and goats. They had to keep moving from place to place to find fresh grass for them. Sometimes arguments broke out between Abraham's servants and Lot's servants over the best fields for the flocks. Abraham wanted these fights to stop. "Let's go off in different directions," he suggested to Lot. "Then there will be plenty for all our animals to eat." When Lot chose the best grassy valleys, Abraham did not mind. God noticed Abraham's kindness. "Look around you," God said to Abraham. "I will give all this land to you and your family."

January 13

Abraham and Sarah longed for a child of their own, but this wasn't possible. They were both very old – Sarah was ninety and Abraham was now ninety-nine years old. But God knew all about the couple's greatest wish. One day, he appeared before Abraham and made him a special promise. "Sarah will have a baby son," said God. "You shall call him Isaac. I will bless you, so that you will have many descendants. I will give you and your family this beautiful country to live in forever. In return for this, you must promise to obey me."

JANUARY 14

ABRAHAM WAS SITTING in his tent when he saw three men walking toward him. It was a very hot day, so Abraham invited the men to rest in the tent. "Stay for something to eat, too," he said. Sarah was preparing their meal when one of the men said to Abraham, "Soon, your wife will have a baby son." Sarah overheard this and burst out laughing. "I'm too old to have a child!" she thought. The man heard her laugh. "Nothing is impossible for God," he said. Suddenly, Abraham and Sarah realized that their guests were not ordinary men. They were messengers sent by God.

JANUARY 15

GOD WAS GOOD to Abraham and Sarah. The following year, Sarah gave birth to a baby boy, just as God had promised. Abraham named him Isaac, which means "he laughs." This was a good name because Isaac was a happy child, and he made his parents laugh with happiness. The name also reminded Sarah of the time she had laughed because she did not believe God's promise of a son. Sarah thanked God for giving her Isaac. "Who would have thought that I would have a baby at my age?" she said. "God has brought great happiness and laughter into our home." Abraham and Sarah adored Isaac.

JANUARY 16

ONE DAY, God wanted to test Abraham's faith. "Take Isaac to the top of that mountain," said God. "Then build an altar and sacrifice your only son to me." Abraham was very sad, but he trusted that God would keep his promises about the future. So he climbed up the mountain and built an altar. Then he tied up Isaac and placed him on top of the altar. But, as Abraham raised his dagger to kill Isaac, God told him to stop. "You have shown that you really do trust in me," said God. So Abraham untied his son. Then he saw a ram entangled in a bush, and he placed the animal on the altar instead of Isaac.

JANUARY 17

THE TIME CAME for Abraham to choose a wife for Isaac. He sent his servant back to the country he had left many years ago. "Find a good match for my son," said Abraham. After a long journey, the servant arrived at Abraham's home town. He stopped by a well and prayed to God. "Let a woman offer me a drink. This will show me she is the right choice for Isaac." A woman came up to him and gave him water from the well. God had answered the servant's prayer. The woman was from Abraham's family, and her name was Rebecca. She agreed to leave her home and marry Isaac.

JANUARY 18

ISAAC REMEMBERED

God's promise to his father that his descendants would become a great nation. So he prayed for Rebecca to have a child. Before long, Rebecca gave birth to twin boys. They were named Esau and Jacob. The brothers were not at all alike. Esau loved being outdoors, hunting deer. He was his father's favorite. Jacob preferred to stay indoors, and his mother loved him best. Esau was the elder son, but God did not want him to become head of the family. One day, Esau sold the rights of a firstborn son to Jacob, just for a bowl of soup. That showed how little Esau cared for God's promise.

JANUARY 19

ISAAC WAS OLD and almost blind. He wanted to give a blessing to his elder son, Esau. "Go out hunting and kill a deer," he said to Esau. "Then make me my favorite stew, and I will bless you with everything I own." Isaac's wife heard what he had said. She went to find Jacob and said to him, "I will cook a stew, so you can give it to your father instead of Esau." Jacob covered himself with goatskin and took the food to Isaac. The old man touched Jacob's hairy arms and said, "You sound like Jacob, but feel like Esau." So Isaac was deceived into thinking he was blessing Esau.

JANUARY 20

SOON ESAU RETURNED

home from the hunt. "I'm back!" he called as he entered Isaac's tent with a bowl of stew. Isaac and Esau soon realized that they had been tricked by Jacob. Esau was furious. "I will kill my cheating brother!" he shouted. When Rebecca heard this, she knew she had to act quickly to save her favorite son. "Let's send Jacob to stay with my brother Laban," Rebecca said to Isaac. So Jacob packed up all his things and said goodbye. He was sad to leave his home, but he had to run away to escape from his brother's anger.

JANUARY 21

JACOB FELT LONELY as he set off on his journey. When night fell, he lay down on the ground to sleep, using a stone for a pillow. Jacob dreamed of a wide stairway reaching up into heaven, with angels going up and down it. God was standing at the top of the stairway. "I am the God of Abraham and Isaac," God said to Jacob. "I am also your God, and I will keep my promise to make your family into a great nation. Wherever you go, I will take care of you." Jacob woke up, full of wonder. "If you bring me home safely, God," prayed Jacob, "I will always obey you."

JANUARY 22

AFTER HIS DREAM,

Jacob felt stronger and happier.
He continued on his way,
searching for his
mother's home town.
Soon he came across
some shepherds
standing by a well.
Jacob asked the men if they knew
his uncle Laban. "Yes, we do," they
replied. "Look, here comes Laban's
daughter, Rachel." Jacob turned
around and saw a beautiful woman
walking toward him. She was leading
a flock of sheep to the well to draw some
water for them. Jacob ran to Rachel and
told her who he was. Together, they
went back to Laban's house.
Laban welcomed Jacob
into his home.

31

JANUARY 23

JACOB BEGAN WORKING for his uncle. "How do you want me to pay you?" asked Laban. "If I work for seven years, I would like to marry your daughter Rachel," replied Jacob. For Jacob, the seven years flew by because he loved Rachel so much. On the evening of the marriage feast, Laban brought his daughter to Jacob. But the next morning, Jacob realized Laban had tricked him. Laban had given his elder daughter, Leah, instead of Rachel. Jacob was angry, but Laban explained that Leah would be sad if her younger sister got married before her. Jacob agreed to marry both sisters and to work seven more years for his uncle.

JANUARY 24

JACOB AND LABAN did not always get along. But Jacob worked hard for his uncle. After twenty years away from home, Jacob decided it was time to return to his father, Isaac. But Laban did not want him to go, so he offered to pay Jacob. Again, Laban tried to cheat Jacob and went back on his promise. God told Jacob to leave. So Jacob set off for home with all his family. Laban came after them. "Let me say goodbye to my daughters and grandchildren," he said. Jacob and Laban made up their quarrel and parted as friends.

JANUARY 25

ON THE JOURNEY back home, Jacob could not stop thinking about his brother. Would his brother still want to kill him? Many years ago, Jacob had played a mean trick on Esau, denying him his birthright. Jacob sent his family and flocks ahead of him, so that he could think alone. As night fell, he prayed to God that his life might be spared and no harm would come to his family.

But then, out of nowhere, a strange man appeared. He came to wrestle with Jacob. "People will call you Israel," said the man as they fought together. "This means you never give up and always believe God's promises." After a long fight, the man left Jacob. He did not tell Jacob his name, but Jacob knew he had met God that night. Through this fight, Jacob's trust in God had been strengthened.

JANUARY 26

THE NEXT MORNING, Jacob caught up with the rest of his family. Then, in the distance, he saw Esau coming toward them with a big crowd of men. Jacob was not only afraid for himself, but also for his wives and their many children. Plucking up all his courage, he went on ahead of his family to meet his brother. What an enormous relief it was when Esau ran up to him and hugged him! Esau had forgiven Jacob for cheating him all those years ago. The twin brothers were so happy to see each other again that they cried for joy.

JANUARY 27

JACOB HAD TWELVE SONS, but Joseph was his favorite. Jacob gave him a special coat to show how much he loved him. This made his older brothers jealous. One day, Joseph began telling his brothers about the strange dreams he had been having. "We were in the fields tying up bundles of corn. My bundle stood up straight, and yours bowed down to mine," said Joseph. "In another dream," said Joseph, "the sun, moon, and eleven stars all bowed down to me." Upon hearing this, the brothers began to hate Joseph more than ever. "Do you really think you can rule over us?" they muttered angrily.

JANUARY 28

ONE DAY, Joseph was sitting at home with Jacob. His brothers were out in the fields, looking after their father's sheep. Jacob was worried because his sons had been away for a long time. "Go and check that they are all safe," he said to Joseph. The brothers saw Joseph from a distance because he was easy to spot in his new, colorful coat. They were so jealous of him that all but one of the brothers wanted to kill him. Jacob's eldest son, Reuben, persuaded his brothers to throw Joseph into a deep pit instead.

JANUARY 29

SOME TRADERS PASSED BY on their way to Egypt to sell their goods. This gave Judah, one of the brothers, an idea. "Let's sell Joseph as a slave, so we can get rid of him and earn some money at the same time," he suggested. So they hauled Joseph out of the pit, took his coat, and sold him to the traders. Then they dipped the coat in goat's blood and took it home to Jacob. "A wild animal must have killed my dearest son!" cried the old man. Jacob was heartbroken.

JANUARY 30

JOSEPH WAS NOT DEAD, but alive and well in Egypt. He was bought as a slave by Potiphar, an officer at the royal palace. Joseph always worked hard, and so Potiphar rewarded him by putting him in charge of his household. Everyone liked Joseph, especially Potiphar's wife. One day, she tried to kiss Joseph, but he pushed her away. This made her angry, so she lied to her husband, saying that it was Joseph who had tried to kiss her. Potiphar was so upset that he had Joseph tied in chains and thrown into prison.

JANUARY 31

IN PRISON, Joseph was joined by the king's baker and chief wine waiter. One morning, the new arrivals looked sad. "Last night I dreamed of a vine with three branches. I squeezed the grapes into the king's cup," said the waiter.

"And I dreamed I was carrying three pastry baskets to the king, but birds came and pecked at them," said the baker. "In three days' time the king will give you back your job," Joseph explained to the waiter. He asked the waiter to mention his name to the king when he was set free. Then he turned to the baker. "But the king will put you to death in three days." It all happened just as Joseph said.

FEBRUARY 1

THE CHIEF wine waiter had promised Joseph that he would remember him to the king. But the waiter forgot all about his friend.

A couple of years later, the king had two strange dreams, and no one could explain their meaning. Then the waiter remembered Joseph and told the king all about him. So Joseph was released from prison and brought before the king. "In my first dream, seven thin cows ate up seven fat cows," said the king. "In the second, seven thin ears of grain ate up seven ripe ears." Joseph explained the meaning of the dreams. "God is warning you that there will be seven years of good harvests, followed by seven years of bad harvests," he said.

FEBRUARY 2

JOSEPH GAVE THE KING

some good advice. "Store up the crops during the seven years of plenty, so there is enough to go around when the harvests fail." The king thought for a moment. "You are a wise man," he said. "I shall make you my prime minister, and then you can put your plans into action."

Everything happened just as Joseph said it would. For the next seven years, storehouses were filled with grain. But then the crops stopped growing, and famine struck.

Joseph made sure all the grain that had been saved was shared among the people.

FEBRUARY 3

JACOB AND HIS SONS

were also affected by the famine. So the brothers traveled to Egypt to buy food. Jacob kept his youngest son, Benjamin, at home. When the brothers came before Joseph, they did not recognize him. But Joseph knew who they were. He wanted to find out what kind of men they had become, so he decided to test them. "You're spies," he said. "No, we're not!" they protested. "Prove your story by bringing your brother back here," ordered Joseph. "I'll keep one of you prisoner."

43

FEBRUARY 4

JACOB DID NOT WANT

Benjamin to go to Egypt, but he had no choice. When the brothers arrived in Egypt, Joseph gave them all the food they needed. The brothers thanked Joseph and started out on their journey home. But, unknown to them, Joseph had planted a silver cup in Benjamin's sack. They had not traveled far when Joseph's servant stopped them. "Who has stolen my master's silver cup?" he demanded. The cup was found in Benjamin's sack. The brothers were taken before Joseph. Judah pleaded for Benjamin. "Punish me instead!" he begged. Now Joseph knew his brothers had changed for the better. "I am Joseph, your long-lost brother!" he cried.

FEBRUARY 5

JOSEPH'S BROTHERS WERE AFRAID

because they had treated Joseph so badly. But Joseph told them not to worry. "It was God's plan that I should come to Egypt," he said. "Go home and bring our father back with you." Jacob could not believe his ears when his sons told him the wonderful news. They packed up their things and set off for Egypt. Joseph came riding out in a royal chariot to greet them. He flung his arms around his father, and both men wept for joy.

45

FEBRUARY 6

THE KING OF EGYPT was worried because there were so many of God's people, known as Israelites, living in his country. He thought that they might form an army to fight against the Egyptians. The king wanted to make sure that this would never happen, so he forced the Israelites to work for him as slaves. He treated them badly and made their lives miserable. But, no matter how hard he made them work, their numbers continued to grow and grow. So many babies were born that the king began to panic. "Throw all the newborn baby boys into the Nile River!" he ordered.

FEBRUARY 7

A WOMAN HAD A BABY SON, and she knew he would be killed if she did not do something to save him. So she made a reed basket and hid him inside. Carefully, she placed the basket in the Nile River. Her older daughter watched from a distance. When the royal princess came to bathe in the river, she found the basket. The baby's sister ran up to the princess. "Let me find a nurse to look after this child for you," she said. Then she got her mother. The baby was cared for by his own mother until he was old enough to live at the palace. The princess adopted him and named him Moses.

FEBRUARY 8

MOSES GREW UP in the palace and was treated like a prince. But he was very sad to see the Israelites slaving away for their Egyptian masters. He knew that he was one of God's people, despite all his fine Egyptian clothes. One day, Moses saw an Egyptian beating a slave, and this threw him into a rage. He killed the Egyptian, then hid his body in the sand. When the king heard what his adopted grandson had done, he was furious and tried to kill Moses. But Moses escaped from the palace and went to live in a country called Midian.

FEBRUARY 9

ONE DAY, Moses was sitting alone by a well. He thought sadly about the past and wondered what the future might hold. Then seven sisters came to the well and began to draw water for their sheep. Soon some shepherds arrived and pushed the sisters out of the way. But Moses helped the women and made sure they got all the water they needed. The sisters told their father what had happened. He was a priest named Jethro, and he invited Moses to live with them. Jethro gave Zipporah, one of his daughters, to Moses as a wife.

FEBRUARY 10

MOSES WORKED AS A SHEPHERD for many years, taking care of the family's flocks. One day, Moses led his sheep to graze on the lower slopes of Mount Sinai. He looked up and saw a strange sight. A bush was on fire, but it did not seem to be burning up in the flames. Suddenly, a voice spoke from the bush. Moses realized it was God's voice. God told Moses that he had seen how unhappy his people were in Egypt. "I am going to rescue my people," said God. "I want you, Moses, to lead them out of Egypt and take them to the beautiful land of Canaan."

FEBRUARY 11

MOSES WAS SURPRISED that God had chosen him for such an important task. "Why have you picked me to lead your people?" he asked. "I'm not special. I don't think anyone will follow me anywhere!" God promised to help Moses, but Moses was still uncertain. "Your brother Aaron will work with you," said God. "I will give you the power to perform miracles, and I will give Aaron the right words to speak to my people." So Moses agreed to return to Egypt and do what God had asked.

FEBRUARY 12

MOSES AND AARON traveled to Egypt, where they met all the leaders of God's people. Aaron

told them about God's promise of freedom. The leaders were happy to hear the news and thanked God for his goodness. Then, Moses and Aaron went to see the king to try to persuade him to let the Israelites leave Egypt.

But the king became very angry when he heard their request. "Your people are just lazy," he shouted. "Now I will make them work even harder. I will never let them go!" So God's people became even more miserable than before.

FEBRUARY 13

GOD TOLD MOSES that he had not forgotten his promise to free his people. But, when Moses and Aaron went back to the palace to talk to the king, he still refused to let the Israelites go. So God turned the waters of the Nile River into blood. But the king would not change his mind. Each time the king refused God's request, God sent a different disaster upon the people of Egypt. Their homes were filled with frogs and huge swarms of gnats and flies. Their animals died, and the Egyptians themselves broke out in painful rashes. Then, a heavy hailstorm flattened their farms. But the king remained as stubborn as ever.

FEBRUARY 14

GOD HAD NOT FINISHED with the people of Egypt. He sent an army of locusts to eat their crops. Then he plunged the country into darkness for three days. God kept his own people safe from all these troubles.

In spite of everything, the king still would not let the Israelites leave Egypt. Moses and Aaron went to see the king one last time. "Unless you let the Israelites go, God will send the most terrible punishment of all upon the Egyptians," warned Moses. "At midnight, the eldest son in every Egyptian home will die." But the king refused to let the Israelites go.

FEBRUARY 15

GOD PROMISED TO KEEP his people safe
from this final disaster. Moses gave instructions so that
every family knew how to protect themselves. Every man
had to kill his best lamb or goat and paint its blood over
the doors and doorposts of the house. This was to make
sure that the angel of death would pass over their homes.
Then a special meal was prepared for the whole family to
eat that evening. Just as God had said would happen, the
firstborn son in every Egyptian family died
that night. But God's people were saved.

February 16

At long last, the king agreed to let Moses lead the Israelites out of Egypt. There was great excitement as they began their journey. But, in spite of everything that had happened, the king soon began to wish he had not let them go. Who would do the hard work now that his slaves had gone? The king sent his soldiers after the Israelites to bring them back to Egypt. The soldiers caught up with them as they were camping by the Red Sea. God's people were trapped! Moses told them not to panic, because God had promised to protect them.

February 17

GOD TOLD MOSES to hold his wooden stick out toward the Red Sea. The crowd watched in astonishment as the waves parted, leaving a path through the waters. Moses led his people across to the other side. The Egyptian soldiers tried to follow them, but the wheels of their chariots got stuck in the sand.

Soon the waves crashed back, drowning the whole army. God looked after his people on their long journey to the new land he had promised them. By day, they were always guided by a tall cloud just ahead of them. Every night, a column of fire showed them God was there.

57

February 18

MOSES LED God's people through the desert. They walked for three days without finding anything to drink. At long last they stumbled upon a place where there was water, but it tasted horrible. The people cried out in despair, and Moses asked God to help them. God showed Moses a piece of wood and told him to throw it into the water. Moses obeyed God, and soon the water was sweet enough to drink. Then God promised his people that, if they obeyed him, he would always take care of them.

FEBRUARY 19

EVERY DAY IN THE DESERT was hot and tiring, and it wasn't long before God's people began to complain. "We were better off in Egypt. At least we weren't hungry there," they moaned. God heard what they were saying and told Moses he would give his people all the food they needed. That evening, a flock of quails settled on the camp. Everyone had plenty of meat to eat. The next morning, the ground was covered with white flakes that tasted sweet, like cookies. Again, there was enough for everyone. The people called the white food "manna." They ate manna for the rest of their long journey.

FEBRUARY 20

GOD'S PEOPLE GRUMBLED a lot on their travels. They found it difficult to believe that God would take care of them. One day, they stopped at a place where there was no water to drink. They were hot and very thirsty. "Why did you bring us here to die of thirst?" they complained to Moses. Some of the people were so angry that they picked up stones to throw at their leader. God told Moses to take his special stick and hit a rock with it. Moses did as he was asked, and water began to flow out from the rock. Soon, there was enough water for everyone to drink.

FEBRUARY 21

JETHRO, Moses' father-in-law, came to visit Moses in the desert. Both men were happy to see each other again. Moses told Jethro about all the wonderful things God had done for his people. Jethro praised God for his great goodness. During his stay, Jethro watched Moses at work. Moses spent every day helping God's people settle their arguments. "Choose some helpers to share this huge task with you," suggested Jethro. "It's too much hard work for one person." Moses was not too proud to listen to advice. He chose a team of wise people to help him guide and teach God's people.

FEBRUARY 22

SEVERAL MONTHS LATER, God's people arrived at Mount Sinai. Moses climbed the holy mountain to pray. God told Moses he was going to speak to him in front of the people, to show them that Moses really was his chosen leader. So the people gathered at the bottom of the mountain. Suddenly, the cloud covering the peak of the mountain changed to fiery smoke, and the ground shook and thunder rumbled. When the people heard God's voice, they were frightened. God said that only Moses could go up the mountain to talk to him. So Moses climbed the holy mountain.

FEBRUARY 23

GOD WANTED his people
to love him and each other.
So he gave special laws to
Moses. These laws were called
the "Ten Commandments."
The laws told the people how to
behave. They must not worship other
gods or make images of them. They must
respect God's name and always obey
their parents. They must not kill, steal
another's husband or wife, or take
something that belonged to
someone else. They must not tell
lies or be jealous of anything,
and they must rest on the
seventh day of the week.
If God's people kept
these laws, they
would live good
and happy lives.

FEBRUARY 24

MOSES SPENT many days talking to God at the top of Mount Sinai. He was gone for so long that the people became impatient. "We need a god to lead us now," they said to Aaron. Aaron told the people to bring him their gold. They did so, and Aaron melted it down to make a statue of a calf. The people worshipped the statue and danced around it. Moses came down from the mountain, carrying two stone slabs with God's commandments written on them. He was so angry at what he saw that he dropped the stone slabs, smashing them into pieces.

FEBRUARY 25

MOSES WAS FURIOUS with Aaron, who had let all this happen while he was away. "I will ask God to forgive you," he said to his people. So, once again, Moses climbed Mount Sinai to talk to God. Trembling with fear, Moses asked God to help him lead his stubborn and sinful people. God was angry with the people, but pleased with his servant Moses. God promised Moses that he would give his people a second chance. "I will never leave my people if they trust and obey me," said God.

FEBRUARY 26

GOD'S PEOPLE were always on the move, so they couldn't build a temple in one place to worship God. But they still needed somewhere special to go to pray. "Make a big tent especially for me," God told Moses. "Use all the best materials. Everybody who wants to can bring gifts to help with the work. When the tent is finished, you can take it with you on your journey." God's people wanted to make the tent as beautiful as possible. They gave fine linen, animal skins, gold, silver, and many other precious things. In the end, Moses had to stop the people from bringing presents, because there was more than enough to make God's tent.

FEBRUARY 27

AT LAST, the people came within sight of Canaan, the Promised Land. So Moses chose twelve men, one from each of the twelve tribes of Israel, to go and discover all they could about Canaan. The spies were gone for six weeks and returned with delicious fruits. But the news they brought back was not good. "This beautiful land will never be ours," they said. "The people are powerful and we will not be able to take over their strong cities."

FEBRUARY 28

YET AGAIN, God's people were unhappy. "Why did we ever leave Egypt?" they grumbled. One of the spies, a man called Caleb, spoke to the crowd. "We must trust in God. Let's get ready to go into the Promised Land!" he said. His friend Joshua agreed with this. But the people were in no mood to listen. They threatened to kill Joshua and Caleb. This made God angry, and he said to Moses, "These people will wander in the desert for forty years. They will never set foot in Canaan. But their children will enter the Promised Land, led by Joshua and Caleb."

FEBRUARY 29

GOD NEVER LEFT his people throughout their long, difficult journey. There were many times when the people made God sad and angry. But there was not a single moment when God stopped caring for his people. During all the years on the move, God made sure his people had food, drink, clothing, and shelter. Above all else, God wanted his people to know he was the Lord their God. He made a solemn promise, which was called his covenant. He promised he would always look after his people in the future, just as he had done in the past. In return, God wanted his people to love and obey him.

March 1

MOSES WAS NOW a very old man. He knew that God wanted a younger leader to take his people into Canaan, the Promised Land. "It is time for you to enter the country that God has promised you," said Moses to the people. "God will go ahead of you and defeat your enemies, so their land will soon be yours. Be brave and remember that God is with you." Then Moses turned to Joshua, his friend and helper. "God wants you to lead his people now," said Moses. "You must always trust in God. Do not be afraid, because God will be with you." Moses realized that the people would be tempted to turn away from God, so he wrote down God's law in a special book and gave it to the priests. "Keep reading this to the people after I have gone," he told the priests. Then Moses sang a beautiful song to the people. It was a reminder of everything that God had done for them.

MARCH 2

THE TIME CAME for Moses to be with God in heaven. Moses was sad that he would never set foot in the country that God had chosen for his people. But God was kind to Moses. He showed Moses a beautiful view of the Promised Land from the top of a mountain. Moses was full of joy when he saw the wonderful country that God was giving to his people, and he died a happy man. Joshua, the new leader that God had chosen, was immediately filled with Moses' wisdom. Right from the start, the people listened to Joshua and obeyed his commands.

MARCH 3

AFTER MOSES HAD DIED, God spoke to Joshua, Moses' assistant. "Get ready to cross over the Jordan River into Canaan, the Promised Land. I will give you the whole country, and no one will be able to stand in your way because I will always be with you, just as I was with Moses. Do not be afraid. If you obey my laws, you will never fail." Joshua told the people what God had said to him. "The time has come to take possession of the land that God has given you," Joshua told them. "Prepare to enter the Promised Land in just three days from now." Everyone was excited and very willing to do as they were asked.

MARCH 4

THREE OF THE TWELVE

tribes of God's people had settled
on the east bank of the Jordan
River. Joshua spoke to these
three tribes. "God has given you this
land, but you must send your best soldiers to help us to
win Canaan," said Joshua. "Your wives and children may
remain on the east bank. When the fighting is over, the
men can return home again across the river." The three
tribes were happy to obey Joshua. They built a big altar to
the east of the river to remind everyone that they belonged
to God's people and worshipped the same great God.

MARCH 5

GOD'S PEOPLE had a problem. Their way into the Promised Land was blocked by the city of Jericho. So Joshua sent two spies into Jericho to find out all they could about the city. Once inside the city walls, the spies entered the house of a woman named Rahab. She was kind and hid the men on the roof of her house so that they would be safe. Soon, some of the king's men knocked on Rahab's door. "You have two spies in your house," they said. "Bring them out at once." But Rahab told them that her visitors had already left and she did not know where they had gone. So, the king's men went off to hunt for the spies.

MARCH 6

THE SPIES ASKED RAHAB why it was she had risked her life to save them. "I know that God will give your people my country," said Rahab. "Now I have done you this favor, I want to ask for a favor in return. When your soldiers take over this city, tell them to spare the lives of my family." The spies told Rahab to hang a red rope out of her window when the army arrived. "This will show our soldiers where you are hiding, and you will all be safe." Rahab thanked the two men. Then, when night fell, she helped them to escape from the city by letting them down a rope tied to her window.

MARCH 7

THE TWO SPIES returned to Joshua and told him everything that had happened. "We know that God will give us this land," they said. So the people prepared to cross the Jordan. The river was very deep and dangerous, but God gave instructions to Joshua to send the priests ahead of the people. The priests were carrying the precious chest that held God's law. As soon as they stepped into the river, the waters stopped flowing! God's people could now walk safely across to the other side.

MARCH 8

THE PRIESTS STOOD in the middle of the river until all the people had gone across. Then Joshua told one man from each of the tribes to take a stone from the riverbed. When the men had done this, the priests stepped onto the riverbank, and the water started to flow again. The twelve men placed the stones together in a tall mound. "In the future, these stones will remind your children how God brought us all safely across the Jordan River and into the Promised Land," said Joshua.

MARCH 9

JOSHUA WAS GAZING at the high walls of Jericho, lost in thought. The city was shut tight against God's people. Suddenly, a man walked up to him, armed with a sword. "Are you one of our soldiers or are you an enemy?" asked Joshua. "I have come to take charge of the Lord's army," answered the stranger. Joshua realized at once that the man was a messenger sent by God. Joshua knew he had to listen to this man and obey his commands, then Jericho would fall into the hands of the Israelites. Joshua was wise and did everything that God's messenger told him to do.

MARCH 10

GOD TOLD JOSHUA to organize a march around the city of Jericho. At the front of the procession were armed soldiers. Then came seven priests blowing on trumpets followed by priests carrying the golden chest. At the back were more armed soldiers. Every day for six days they marched once around the city to the sound of trumpet blasts. On the seventh day, Joshua told the group to circle the city seven times and to raise a battle cry on the last lap. When Joshua gave the signal, the people began to shout, and the city walls crashed to the ground.

MARCH 11

THE PEOPLE OF CANAAN saw the defeat of Jericho and were afraid for their lives. Not far from Jericho was the city of Gibeon. The people living there tried to trick Joshua. They went to see him, dressed in tatters. "We have come from far away," they lied. "Please accept us as your friends." So, Joshua made peace with them. But, when he discovered the truth, he was furious. He had promised not to harm them, but he still wanted to punish them. So he made them serve God's people as woodcutters and water carriers.

MARCH 12

AFTER MANY LONG BATTLES, God's people were at last able to settle down in the land of Canaan. Some parts of the land were good for growing crops, while other parts were not so fertile. It was Joshua's job to divide all the land fairly among the twelve different groups that made up God's people.

The land that each group, or tribe, received was a precious gift from God. When all the land had been divided up, Joshua set apart some special towns. Any person who killed someone accidentally could flee to one of these towns and live there, safe from revenge attacks.

MARCH 13

WHEN THE LAND of Canaan was divided up between the tribes, there was one tribe that did not receive a share. This tribe was called the Levites. These people had been chosen by God for a special purpose. God wanted them to serve as his holy priests. They would not have time for God's work if they had to farm the land. So Joshua ordered the other eleven tribes to hand over some of their crops and cities to the Levites. The other tribes did so happily. So the Levites always had enough to live on and could spend all their time doing God's work.

MARCH 14

WHEN THE TASK of dividing the land was complete, Joshua called together the leaders of the twelve tribes. "God has kept all his promises to you, the descendants of Abraham. You have come to live in the beautiful land that God has given you. Now you must promise to serve your God." So, there and then, the leaders made a solemn promise that their people would always obey God. Joshua put up a big stone in a holy place, to help the people remember their promise.

MARCH 15

JOSHUA LED GOD'S PEOPLE until the day he died. Without a new leader, the people tried to follow God, but they soon began to disobey him. They did not teach their children about God, so their children started to worship idols. Soon, the people forgot all about the great things God had done for them.

This made God very sad and angry. He let the original tribes of Canaan rise up and rule over his people. But God never stopped loving them. He sent leaders, called judges, to guide them and remind them of his laws.

MARCH 16

FOR EIGHTEEN YEARS, God's people were ruled by King Eglon of Moab. Eglon made them so miserable that they cried out to God for help. God chose a man named Ehud to be their leader. Ehud was left-handed and used this to his advantage. He went to see King Eglon, hiding a sharp dagger on his right side. Ehud told the king that he had a secret message for him. The king didn't suspect any danger, so he invited Ehud to a private meeting. As soon as the two men were alone, Ehud drew his dagger with his left hand. "I have a message from God for you!" he said, and killed the king.

MARCH 17

GOD'S PEOPLE lived in peace for eighty years after Ehud saved them from King Eglon. But, when Ehud died, the people forgot about God again. As before, this led to great unhappiness for God's people. They were attacked and ruled over by a king named Jabin. He treated them very cruelly. After twenty years of misery, they begged God for help. At that time, the leader of God's people was a wise woman named Deborah. God told Deborah to send for an army general named Barak. This man would help God's people win another amazing battle.

March 18

Barak asked Deborah to go with him to battle, and she agreed. Deborah told Barak to gather ten thousand soldiers. The commander of King Jabin's army was a man named Sisera. He had nine hundred iron chariots and led a huge army, so he was not afraid of Barak's men. God told Deborah the right time to attack Sisera's army, who were camped by a river. Deborah gave the order, and Barak's army charged down a hillside, surprising the enemy below. Barak's soldiers killed all of Sisera's troops, but Sisera escaped and hid in the tent of a woman named Jael. But Jael was loyal to Barak. So, when Sisera slept, Jael killed him with a tent stake.

MARCH 19

SOON GOD'S PEOPLE were in trouble again with a new enemy, the Midianites. This fierce desert tribe did not attack the people. But they stole all their crops and animals, so there was nothing left to eat. After seven years of terrible raids, the people begged for God's help. God chose Gideon, a simple farmer, to lead the fight against the Midianites. "Do not be afraid, I will help you beat your enemies," God told Gideon. But Gideon needed a little persuading. "I'm no hero!" he told God. "How can I be sure that you really have chosen me for this task?"

MARCH 20

GIDEON WAS A MODEST MAN. He didn't feel he was important enough to lead the Israelites. He needed proof that it was really God who had talked to him. So, he laid a sheepskin on the ground. "If this fleece is damp with dew tomorrow morning, even though the ground is dry, I will know you have chosen me," he said to God. The next day Gideon found that this had happened. Then he asked for one last sign. "Tomorrow, if the fleece stays dry, even though the ground is wet with dew, I will be convinced."

When Gideon found the ground wet and the fleece dry, he had all the proof he needed. Full of confidence and faith, he led God's people against the Midianites.

89

March 21

THOUSANDS OF MEN volunteered to join Gideon's army. "You don't need so many soldiers," God told Gideon. "Trust me to help you win." So Gideon picked just three hundred men. Late one night, Gideon's men crept down to the enemy camp, carrying trumpets, pots, and torches. When Gideon gave the signal, they all blew their trumpets and smashed their pots. Then they shouted as loud as they could and held up their torches. The Midianites thought they were surrounded by a huge army. They fled in terror, and the battle was won.

MARCH 22

GOD'S PEOPLE were unhappy once again. The Philistines, a new and powerful enemy, were making their lives a misery. Among the Israelites was a good man named Manoah. He longed for God to save his people. One day, God told Manoah's wife that she was going to have a baby boy, who would grow up to lead the fight against the Philistines. This was a great surprise, for the couple was old. When the baby arrived, he was named Samson. He never had his hair cut from the day he was born. This was to show that he had been set apart to serve God.

MARCH 23

SAMSON GREW UP to be incredibly strong. He also grew up to be a big problem to the Philistines. By the time Samson was a young man, he had already won many battles against the Philistines single-handed. One day, Samson met a young Philistine woman named Delilah. She was very beautiful, and Samson fell in love with her. But Delilah was also very greedy. When the Philistines offered her money to find out the secret of Samson's amazing strength, she set out to trick Samson into telling her. Three times Samson gave her the wrong answer and made a fool of her. But in the end her nagging wore him down. "If my head were shaved, I would be as weak as any man," he said. Delilah wasted no time. As soon as Samson fell asleep, she let the Philistines shave off his hair.

MARCH 24

WHEN SAMSON woke up, he tried to fight his enemies, but his strength had gone. The Philistines blinded him and threw him into jail. They held a party to celebrate and brought in Samson to jeer at him. Samson's hair was beginning to grow again, and he prayed to God to give him his strength back. "Let me die with the Philistines," he shouted, and pushed against the pillars that held up the building. The building crashed to the ground, killing everyone.

MARCH 25

NAOMI LIVED in Bethlehem with her husband and two sons. One year, the harvest was so bad that the family nearly starved. They packed up their things and traveled to a nearby country, where there was plenty to eat. Not long afterward, Naomi's husband died. Her two sons married local women and brought them home to take care of Naomi. Then tragedy struck again. Both sons died, leaving Naomi alone in a foreign land. The widows of Naomi's sons were named Ruth and Orpah. They did their best to comfort their mother-in-law. But soon Naomi became homesick and decided to return to her own country. "We'll come with you!" Ruth and Orpah said to Naomi.

MARCH 26

THE THREE WOMEN set off on their journey. Naomi was very grateful to her daughters-in-law for their kindness, but she didn't want to be a burden to them. She turned to her companions. "Go home now," she urged them. "Get married again while you are still young." Orpah hugged Naomi and said goodbye to her. But Ruth refused to leave her. "Let me stay!" Ruth begged. "Wherever you go, I will go." Naomi realized that Ruth would not change her mind, so they traveled on together. Before long, they arrived back at Naomi's home town of Bethlehem.

MARCH 27

IN THOSE DAYS, women could not earn money to buy food, so Ruth went out to gather scraps in the fields. It was harvest time, and she hoped to find enough barley to live on for a while. As Ruth was working, the owner of the field spotted her. His name was Boaz, and he had heard how Ruth had been good to her mother-in-law. He decided to show her kindness in return. "If you are thirsty, drink the water from the jars in the fields," Boaz said to Ruth. Then he ordered his workers to leave extra barley behind them in the fields. This meant that Ruth picked up plenty to take home.

MARCH 28

NAOMI WAS AMAZED

when Ruth arrived home with her basket full of barley. Ruth explained what had happened, and Naomi clapped her hands for joy. "God is good to us!" she said. "Boaz is one of our relatives!" Naomi soon thought of a plan. "Find Boaz when he is alone," she told Ruth. "Ask him to help us because we belong to his family." Ruth did as she was told. Boaz agreed to buy the land that was owned by Naomi's family. Then he married Ruth and took Naomi into his home. To Naomi's delight, Ruth gave birth to a son. Ruth's kindness had brought new happiness into Naomi's life.

March 29

Hannah was very sad

because she had no children. Her husband, a man named Elkanah, had another wife. Her name was Peninnah, and she had many sons and daughters.

Peninnah made Hannah even more unhappy by boasting about her family. Once a year, Elkanah took them all to worship God in a holy place called Shiloh. During a special feast, Hannah felt so left out she could bear it no longer. She slipped away and went to the temple. Tears rolled down her cheeks as she prayed to God. "If you give me a child," she sobbed, "I promise I will give him back to serve you all his life."

MARCH 30

ELI, THE TEMPLE PRIEST, saw Hannah. He went over and asked her what was the matter. "I am very upset," said Hannah. "I have been asking God for help." Eli felt sorry for her. "May God answer your prayers," he said kindly. When Hannah returned home, she found to her joy that she was expecting a baby. But she did not forget her promise to God. She had a son and named him Samuel. When Samuel was still a small child, Hannah brought him to Shiloh. Eli took him on to be his special helper at the temple.

MARCH 31

ELI AND SAMUEL spent all their time in the temple. One night, Samuel was woken up by someone calling his name. Thinking that Eli must need him, he went to his friend. "I did not ask for you," said Eli. "Go back to bed." But Samuel heard the voice again. The third time Samuel came to him, Eli realized that it was God calling Samuel. "Listen to what God is saying to you," he told the boy. After that night, God spoke to Samuel many times. In years to come, Samuel was to become a great prophet, passing on messages from God to his people.

APRIL 1

THE PHILISTINES

were attacking God's people, the Israelites, and winning victories over them. The leaders of Israel came up with an idea. "Let's take God's golden chest to war with us!" they said. "Then we shall beat our enemies." The holy chest held God's laws, and they thought this would give them victory. But, when the Philistines saw the golden chest on the battlefield, they fought harder than ever. Israel lost more than thirty-thousand soldiers, including Eli's two sons. Worst of all, the Philistines captured the holy chest and took it away to their camp.

APRIL 2

THE PHILISTINES were pleased with their new possession. They believed they had won power over God. They took the golden chest to a temple and placed it next to the statue of Dagon, a Philistine god. The next morning, visitors to the temple found Dagon's statue lying face down in front of God's holy chest. They picked up the statue and put it back in its place. But, the same thing happened the next day, and this time the statue was broken into pieces! This convinced the Philistines that God was angry with them, so they sent the chest back to be with the people of Israel.

APRIL 3

GOD'S PEOPLE loved Samuel and were happy to be led by him. But, when Samuel grew old, the people began to think about what the future might hold. At a big meeting, they spoke to Samuel about their worries. "We want a king," they demanded. Samuel was upset, feeling unwanted after all the years he had spent serving the people. But God told Samuel that the people were not rejecting him as their leader, they just did not want to be ruled by God any more. "Let my people have their way. Give them a king, even though things will not turn out quite as they expect them to," God said to Samuel.

APRIL 4

SAUL WAS THE SON of a farmer. He was striking to look at, being a head taller than anyone else. The young man was always happy to help his father.

One day, some of his father's donkeys wandered off and got lost. His father sent Saul out with one of the servants to look for them. They searched high and low for three days, and Saul began to give up hope of ever finding the animals. "Let's go home before my father starts to worry," he said to his servant. But the servant had another idea. "We're not far from where Samuel lives," he said. "Let's visit him, to see if he can help us find the lost donkeys." On their way to Samuel's house, they were met by the great man himself.

April 5

GOD HAD TOLD SAMUEL he was about to meet the future king of Israel. As soon as Samuel saw the tall young man, he knew that Saul was the one God had been speaking about. Before Saul could ask Samuel about the lost donkeys, Samuel told him they had already been found. Then he surprised Saul again by inviting him to be guest of honor at a special feast. The morning after the feast, just as Saul was about to leave, Samuel spoke to him in private. "God's people want a king, and God has chosen you to be the people's king," he said. Then Samuel took a flask and sprinkled olive oil over Saul's head, as a sign that God had chosen him to be the first king of Israel.

April 6

Samuel gathered God's people together, so he could tell them who was going to be their king. He called Saul's name. Everyone looked around, but Saul was nowhere to be seen. Nervous of standing in front of such a big crowd, Saul had tried to hide. A search began, and Saul was soon found. "Here is your king!" cried Samuel, and the crowd cheered. Samuel wrote down a list of rules for the new king of Israel to follow. Above all, Saul must always remember to obey God.

APRIL 7

SAUL ENJOYED leading his army into war. He was successful as long as he listened to Samuel, who told him what God wanted him to do. But, before long, Saul began to think he could manage alone.

One day, he was preparing his soldiers for battle when Samuel sent him a message. "Wait a week for me to come, before you start to fight," was Samuel's request. But Saul became impatient, and disobeyed Samuel's instructions. Samuel was furious when he arrived. "You have disobeyed God," he said to Saul. "Now your sons will not rule after you. God will find a new king from another family."

April 8

SAMUEL WAS SAD, because Saul had turned out to be a bad king. "Go to Bethlehem and visit Jesse," God told Samuel. "I want one of his sons to become the next king." Samuel went to see Jesse, who introduced him to seven of his sons. God told Samuel to turn each young man away. He made it clear that, so far, Samuel had not met the chosen one. "Have you any more sons?' Samuel asked Jesse. "My youngest boy, David, is in the fields, feeding the sheep," answered the old man. As soon as Samuel saw David, he knew his search was over. He sprinkled oil on David's head to show that he had been chosen by God.

APRIL 9

IT WAS MANY YEARS before David became king. Meanwhile, Saul continued to rule Israel and fight against the Philistines. Saul did not always win his battles, because he lacked trust in God. But Saul's son Jonathan believed that God could give them victory over their enemies, whatever the odds. One day, Jonathan and his servant attacked a group of Philistine soldiers who were guarding a mountain pass. There were just the two of them against many. But God sent an earthquake to help Jonathan, and the whole Philistine army ran away in panic.

APRIL 10

KING SAUL was not a happy man. He had turned away from God and sometimes fell into terrible moods. "I know just the thing to help you," said one of Saul's servants. "Jesse has a son named David, who plays the harp beautifully. Perhaps his music would cheer you up." Saul liked this idea, so he sent for David. Saul grew to like the shepherd boy from Bethlehem. His tunes on the harp always comforted Saul when he felt gloomy. Saul told Jesse that he was very pleased with David and wanted him to live at the palace. So David moved in and played soothing music whenever he was asked to by the bad-tempered king.

APRIL 11

EVERYONE STOPPED to listen when David played his harp and sang. He wrote some wonderful poems, which he set to music. These songs are known as psalms, and many of them give praise to God. David was thinking about his time as a shepherd when he composed one of his most

famous psalms. "The Lord is my shepherd, I shall not want," sang David. In this psalm, he compares God to a shepherd taking care of his flock. We are the sheep, and God gives us everything we need. He helps us to live pure and peaceful lives, and he comforts us when bad things happen to us.

APRIL 12

KING SAUL'S ARMY was at war with the Philistines. All the king's soldiers were afraid of one man in the enemy camp, a giant named Goliath. Every morning and evening, Goliath bellowed out the same challenge, "If one of you can beat me, my army will serve your king. But, if your man loses, you will all be our slaves." David was only a young boy, but he wanted to fight Goliath. He went to see King Saul. "I know I'm small, but I can win, because God is on our side," he said boldly. He persuaded the king to let him take on Goliath.

APRIL 13

KING SAUL gave David his suit of armor, but it was too big for him to wear. "I shall do this my way," David said. He ran to a stream and picked out five stones. Then he went to find his enemy. Goliath laughed and laughed when he saw David. But David stood his ground. "My God will help me to win," he said. Then he swung his sling and aimed a stone straight at Goliath. It hit Goliath between the eyes, and the giant fell to the ground. David grabbed Goliath's sword and killed him with it. When the Philistines saw that their hero was dead, they fled in terror.

APRIL 14

DAVID WAS VERY POPULAR with the people after his amazing victory over Goliath. King Saul started to feel jealous of David, realizing that God was with him. The royal court was no longer a safe place for David. But David still had one good friend at court. Saul's son Jonathan was a brave soldier, just like David. The pair loved each other like brothers. One day, Jonathan gave David his sword, bow, and belt as a sign of their strong friendship. "We will always be friends, whatever may happen in the future," they promised each other.

April 15

Saul kept sending David to fight against the Philistines, secretly hoping he would be killed in battle. But each time David returned victorious – and more popular than ever. Soon, Saul's jealousy grew to hatred, and he ordered his men to kill David. Jonathan begged his father to spare David's life. "Think of all the great battles he has won," said Jonathan. "Perhaps he doesn't deserve to die," agreed Saul. So for a while David was safe again. But then, one day, when David was playing his harp, Saul threw his spear at him in a fit of jealously. David now realized his life was in danger.

APRIL 16

SAUL WAS DETERMINED to kill David. One night he sent his men to David's house. "Wait till morning, then go in and kill him," he ordered. David's wife Michal was Saul's daughter, and she found out about her father's plan. "You must escape tonight!" she warned David. She helped him slip out of a back window. Then she dressed a dummy to look like David and put it in his bed. When Saul's men came looking for David, Michal said he was ill. Saul was furious when he found out David had escaped.

APRIL 17

DAVID HAD AN INVITATION to dine with Saul, but he didn't trust the king. So, he went to see his old friend Jonathan to find out whether Saul still meant to harm him. "How will you tell me what you learn?" asked David. "Wait here in the fields," replied Jonathan. "I will come back to practice with my bow and arrow. If my father still wants to kill you, I will call out 'The arrow is further on!' Then you will know." Jonathan went to speak to his father and found that he had not changed his mind. So Jonathan got the message to David in the way they had agreed, and they parted with great sorrow.

APRIL 18

DAVID WAS NOW in great danger. He could not go back to the king's court. So he went into hiding and traveled from place to place. Then, one day, he came across a huge cave. It was a safe hiding place. David was still a popular hero, so word soon got around about his cave. Hundreds of people came to join him there. Many who came were discontented with their lives, and they wanted David to be their leader. So David took them in and set up headquarters in the cave.

APRIL 19

SAUL WAS STILL SEARCHING for David so that he could kill him. One day, as David and his men were resting at the back of the cave, King Saul himself stepped into their hideout. This was the perfect chance for David to get rid of his enemy. Instead, David crept up to Saul and cut a strip off his robe. Then he followed Saul out of the cave. "Look at me!" David shouted, waving the cloth at Saul. "I could have killed you just now, but I didn't. Can't we make peace?" Saul was embarrassed by David's kindness, and so he left him alone.

April 20

DURING SHEEP-SHEARING time, David protected the shepherds of a farmer named Nabal. One day, David heard that Nabal was preparing a feast for the shepherds, so he sent messengers to ask Nabal for any leftovers. Nabal refused David's request, and this made David very angry. "Is this the thanks I get for taking care of his men?" he fumed. He was about to lead an attack on Nabal when the farmer's wife, Abigail, arrived. She brought food and wine as a peace offering and persuaded David not to kill her husband. Soon afterward, Nabal died, and David asked Abigail to marry him.

APRIL 21

KING SAUL HATED DAVID for the rest of his life. Saul died fighting his old enemy, the Philistines. Saul's son Jonathan died in the same battle. Only when Saul was dead was it safe for David to return to Israel. God told David to go to the south of the country, where the people welcomed him and made him king. But Saul's only living son, Ish-Bosheth, became king of the northern part of Israel. Fights broke out between the armies serving David and Ish-Bosheth. After many battles, Ish-Bosheth was killed. At long last, the twelve tribes of Israel asked David to rule over the whole land.

121

APRIL 22

AFTER DAVID became king of Israel, he chose Jerusalem as the country's new capital. Jerusalem was a strong fortress city, ruled by a tribe called the Jebusites. The Jebusites laughed at David because they thought nobody could get into their city. David realized he would have to outwit the Jebusites. He ordered some men to climb up the steep tunnels that carried water supplies into Jerusalem. "Once you are inside the city, open the gates to let the rest of us in," David told the men. So, David's army captured Jerusalem in a surprise attack. Jerusalem became known as "David's city."

April 23

THE PHILISTINES hated David. They had never forgiven him for killing their hero Goliath all those years ago. When the Philistines heard that David was the new king of Israel, they gathered together their entire army to track him down. Now that David had grown so powerful, they wanted to get their revenge at last. They vowed to kill King David. But David was not at all frightened by the Philistines' show of force. He asked God what to do. "Go and attack your old enemies," God told David. "I will hand them over to you." David listened to God and obeyed his commands. So, God was with David, and he finally crushed the Philistine army once and for all.

APRIL 24

DAVID DID NOT FORGET to thank God for his great goodness. He knew he had become king and defeated the Philistines only because it was God's plan for him to do so. David wanted Jerusalem to be God's holy city. So he gave an order for the chest holding God's laws to be brought to the city. There was much celebration as the golden chest was carried through the streets. David led the procession, dancing and singing in praise to God.

The chest was placed in a special tent, and David handed out food to the cheering crowds.

APRIL 25

DAVID NEVER FORGOT

his dear friend Jonathan, the son of King Saul. Before they parted for the last time, David told Jonathan he would take care of his family when he became king. Now it was time to keep that promise. David asked his servants if any of Saul's family were still alive. Jonathan had been killed by the Philistines, but his son Mephibosheth had survived. Mephibosheth had been unable to walk since the time of his father's death. So, David sent for Jonathan's son and invited him to live at the palace. He treated him like his own son. Mephibosheth was very grateful and returned David's kindness with lifelong loyalty.

April 26

It was springtime, and David's armies were away at war. David himself had stayed at home. One afternoon, David looked down from his roof garden and saw a beautiful woman. She was bathing in a nearby courtyard. "What is that woman's name?" he asked his servant. "Bathsheba," replied the man. "She is married to one of your best soldiers." David knew it was wrong to steal another man's wife, but he ordered Bathsheba to come to his palace. A short time later, Bathsheba told David she was pregnant. So David sent her husband to fight a dangerous battle. He was soon killed, and David was free to marry Bathsheba.

APRIL 27

TIME PASSED, and Bathsheba gave birth to a son. God was not happy with David and sent a holy man named Nathan to his palace. Nathan told David a story. "Two men lived in a town. One was rich and the other poor. The rich man had everything he needed, but he took the only thing the poor man really loved – his pet lamb. He killed it and served it to his guests." David was disgusted. "But you are like that rich man," said Nathan. "You stole Bathsheba from her husband, and she was all he had in the world." David felt ashamed and begged God for forgiveness.

April 28

David's son Absalom

was very handsome. He was also desperate to be the next king of Israel. But Absalom did not want to wait until his father died. So, he spent a lot of time with the people, getting to know them and helping to settle their quarrels. He wanted to become more popular than David, so he could lead a rebellion against him. The king was the last to hear about his son's plot. By the time David realized what was going on, even his closest friends had joined Absalom's side. David was very sad, but he knew he had to leave Jerusalem before Absalom and his followers took over the city.

APRIL 29

WHEN DAVID LEFT

Jerusalem, the priests left too, and they took God's holy chest with them. But, despite Absalom's treachery, David did not stop trusting God.
So he made sure that the chest was returned to the city. "If God still wants me to be king, he will return me safely to Jerusalem, too," he said. There were many battles between the supporters of David and Absalom. David did not want his son harmed, but Absalom was killed. David was heartbroken, but he knew it was God's will. So, David returned to Jerusalem in triumph.

APRIL 30

WHEN KING DAVID GREW OLD, the people began to wonder who would be their next leader.

Adonijah was David's oldest living son, and he was eager to take over as king. So he held a feast with his supporters and declared himself the country's new ruler. But not everyone liked Adonijah. Many preferred his younger brother Solomon. When Nathan the prophet heard what Adonijah had done, he rushed to tell the king. David was furious that Adonijah had declared himself king without his knowledge. He called for Bathsheba, Solomon's mother. "Our son Solomon shall be the next king," he promised. Then David sent Zadok the priest to a place called Gihon to anoint Solomon king.

MAY 1

WHEN SOLOMON first became king, David was able to give him lots of good advice. But, before long, the old man died, and Solomon was left with all the work and worry of ruling Israel on his own. One night, Solomon had a dream in which God spoke to him. "What gift would you like me to give you?" asked God. Solomon replied without hesitation. "What I need most of all is wisdom," he said. "I can't guide the people without your help." God was very pleased with Solomon's answer. So he rewarded Solomon with riches and good health, as well as the wisdom he had asked for.

131

MAY 2

KING SOLOMON soon had a chance to test his gift of wisdom. One day, two women came to see him, bringing a baby boy with them. Each woman claimed that the child belonged to her. They wanted Solomon to settle their argument. Solomon took the baby and asked for a sword. "If I cut the boy in two, then you can have half each," he said to the women. "Yes," said one of the women. "That's a good idea!" But the other woman was horrified. "Don't harm the boy! I would rather give the child away, than see him die!" At once Solomon knew this woman must be the true mother, and he gave the baby back to her. Solomon was soon known far and wide for his wise judgment.

MAY 3

ALL THE TIME David was king of Israel, he was too busy fighting wars to build a temple of worship to God. Now that there was peace, this important task fell to his son Solomon. The young king made plans to build the most beautiful temple that the world had ever seen. Solomon used only the very finest materials. He employed thousands of workers to saw timber, cut and shape stone, and cast metals. Once the temple was built, it was decorated with gold and precious jewels. After seven long years of hard work, the spectacular building was finished at last. Then Solomon brought the golden chest holding God's holy laws and placed it in the center of the temple.

May 4

The reign of King Solomon was a time of peace and prosperity. God kept his promise to Solomon and gave him amazing riches, as well as wisdom. Solomon built a fantastic palace, called the Palace of the Forest of Lebanon. It was an enormous building – big enough to house all his seven hundred wives! Everything in the palace was made from gold and other precious materials. He built the throne hall in fine cedar wood, from floor to ceiling. This was the Hall of Justice, where he was judge. But the most splendid thing of all was King Solomon's throne. Six steps led up to the gold and ivory seat, with two lions at each end of every step. Nothing like it had ever been seen before.

May 5

STORIES OF SOLOMON'S wealth and wisdom soon began to reach the courts of kings and queens in distant lands. The queen of Sheba decided to find out whether these tales were really true. So she set off to visit Solomon, leading a long procession of camels carrying expensive gifts. When she arrived at Solomon's palace and saw the incredible riches, she couldn't believe her eyes! The queen asked Solomon many difficult questions, and she found he was as wise as he was rich. She left for home, impressed with all she had seen and heard.

MAY 6

WHEN SOLOMON grew old, he turned away from God. His many foreign wives led him astray, and he began to worship their gods. So God decided to divide Israel in two, making one part much bigger than the other. God said that Solomon's son Rehoboam would rule over the smaller part of the country. He chose Jeroboam, an official of Solomon's court, to rule the larger share of land. But, when Solomon died, Rehoboam became king of all Israel. This was not what God wanted. Rehoboam announced he was going to be very strict, and the people rebelled. "We want Jeroboam to rule us!" they cried. So Rehoboam was banished to the south, where he reigned over a tiny kingdom called Judah. Jeroboam became king of the rest of Israel. So, the country was divided just as God had said.

MAY 7

JEROBOAM WAS A BAD KING, and he encouraged the people to worship false gods. One day, Jeroboam's son became very ill. The king told his wife to visit a prophet named Ahijah to find out if he would get better. The king's wife disguised herself as a peasant woman and traveled to the prophet's house. Ahijah was old and blind, but God told him who his visitor was. "Stop trying to trick me!" he said. Then he told her God was going to punish the king for his wicked ways. "Not only will your son die," said Ahijah. "But disaster will fall on the whole royal family."

MAY 8

EVERYTHING THAT AHIJAH said to Jeroboam's wife came true. King Jeroboam died and, soon afterward, every member of his family was killed. There followed a very dark time for God's people. The kings that ruled after Jeroboam built temples and shrines to false gods. Soon the people began to forget about the one true God. The worst ruler of all was King Ahab. He made God very angry and sad. Ahab's wicked wife, Queen Jezebel, worshipped a foreign god called Baal. She wanted to make Baal-worship the religion of Israel.

MAY 9

GOD DID NOT ABANDON his people. He chose a holy man named Elijah to be his special prophet and bring the people back to him. Elijah lived a simple life of prayer, and he hated Baal-worship. He went to see King Ahab and told him God was angry at the way he was ruling the country. "There will be no more rain until I, God's messenger, give the command," said Elijah. For the next few years, there was almost nothing to eat or drink in the land of Israel. But God sent ravens to bring food to Elijah and showed him a stream where he could drink.

MAY 10

GOD TOLD ELIJAH to go to a place called Zarephath. "A widow who lives there will take care of you," said God. When Elijah met the woman, he asked her for some water and bread. She looked at him sadly. "I only have enough flour and oil to make one small loaf for my son, then we will both starve," she said. "Make a loaf for me first," said Elijah. "Then make another for yourself. God will never let you go hungry again." Elijah went to the woman's house, where she made him the loaf. From that day on, there was always flour in the jar and the oil never dried up.

MAY 11

SOME TIME LATER, the widow's son became ill and died. The boy's mother was beside herself with grief and blamed Elijah. "How could you let this happen?" she sobbed. "What have you got against me?" "Give your son to me," said Elijah. He took the boy and carried him upstairs. Then he prayed for the boy to come back to life again. God heard Elijah's prayer, and the boy woke up, as if from a deep sleep. The boy's mother was overjoyed. "Now I know for certain that you have been sent by God," she said to Elijah.

MAY 12

THREE YEARS of drought did not make King Ahab and Queen Jezebel change their evil ways. They killed God's prophets and replaced them with prophets of Baal. So Elijah challenged King Ahab to a contest. "Let's see who worships the true God!" he said. The king and his prophets met Elijah at the top of a mountain. Elijah told the prophets to pray to Baal to light their altar. They prayed and prayed, but nothing happened. Then Elijah poured water over his altar and asked God to set it on fire. The next moment flames were leaping from the drenched altar. When the people saw this, they killed the prophets of Baal.

MAY 13

KING AHAB HURRIED BACK to the palace to tell Queen Jezebel what had happened. She was furious and swore to kill Elijah. The terrified prophet ran for his life. He ran for forty days and forty nights. Finally, he stopped to rest in a cave. He could hear the sound of raging winds, and he felt the ground shake beneath his feet. Outside, he saw a fire sweeping across a hillside. Then, all was calm, and God spoke to Elijah. "Go back and continue your work for me. Don't be afraid. I will take good care of you."

MAY 14

GOD KNEW that Elijah needed a friend to help him. A prophet's life could be difficult and very lonely. "Go and look for a young man named Elisha," God told Elijah. "He will be your helper and will continue your work after you have gone." Elijah found Elisha plowing his father's fields. At once, Elisha knew that he had to follow Elijah. "Let me kiss my parents goodbye, then I will come with you," he said. Elisha knew there was no turning back. He killed the oxen that had pulled his plow and burned the plow to cook the meat. Then he gave the food to his friends and family as a parting gift.

MAY 15

CLOSE TO KING AHAB'S PALACE was a vineyard, which was owned by a man named Naboth. King Ahab wanted this vineyard for himself, so he could turn it into a vegetable garden. He offered to pay for the land, but Naboth refused to sell. "The land belongs to my family," he insisted. Ahab lay in bed sulking and refusing to eat. So, Queen Jezebel plotted to murder Naboth.

She wrote to the city leaders, ordering them to accuse Naboth of cursing God and the king. No one dared to disobey Jezebel, so Naboth was falsely accused and put to death. God sent Elijah to see King Ahab. "God will punish you for what you have done," warned Elijah.

145

MAY 16

KING AHAB made plans to attack a neighboring country. He wanted to win back land that belonged to Israel. He asked King Jehoshaphat, who ruled the kingdom of Judah, to join him in the fight. "I will help you, but first ask God whether the time is right to start a battle," advised Jehoshaphat. Ahab called together his prophets. They all agreed that their king would win a great victory. Only one prophet thought differently. His name was Micaiah.

"An evil spirit put lies in the mouths of these prophets," said Micaiah. "If you go to war, God will bring disaster upon you," he warned Ahab.

146

MAY 17

KING AHAB had never listened to God before, and he wasn't about to start now. He was furious with Micaiah for his gloomy warning. "You never have anything good to say about me!" shouted King Ahab. Then he had Micaiah thrown into prison. Soon afterward, the two kings went off to fight. King Jehoshaphat wore his royal robes, but King Ahab put on a disguise, so he would not be recognized. Then he followed his soldiers in a chariot. God's patience finally ran out with Ahab. During the battle, an arrow struck Ahab and killed him. King Jehoshaphat survived. He was a good king and did everything he could to please God.

MAY 18

ELIJAH THE PROPHET was out walking with Elisha, his helper. Elisha had a strong feeling that this would be his last day with Elijah. Three times, the old prophet asked Elisha to let him walk on by himself. But, each time, Elisha refused to leave his master. Finally, they came to the Jordan River. Elijah rolled up his cloak and struck the water. The water divided, and they crossed over on dry ground. Then Elijah turned to his young helper. "Is there anything special you would like me to give you before I go?" asked Elijah. Elisha thought for a moment. "I would like you to pass on your greatness and power," he said.

MAY 19

ELIJAH GAVE a strange
reply. "If you see me when I go,
you will get your wish," he said.
Suddenly, a chariot of fire appeared,
pulled by golden horses. The burning
chariot swept Elijah away and carried
him up to heaven in a whirlwind. Elisha
called out after Elijah, but he had already
disappeared. Elijah's cloak lay on the ground.
Elisha picked it up and sadly retraced his steps
to the Jordan River. He wondered whether
God would give him what he had asked for.
When he got to the riverbank, he rolled up
Elijah's cloak and struck the water with it.
The water immediately parted, and Elisha
knew that Elijah's power had come to him.

MAY 20

A GROUP OF PROPHETS were watching as Elisha parted the waters of the Jordan River. "Look how Elijah's spirit has come to rest on Elisha," they said. News soon spread that Elisha had taken over the work of Elijah. When Elisha went to stay in Jericho, some worried men came to see him. "There is something wrong with our water," they said. "It makes us ill and kills our crops." God told Elisha to sprinkle salt into the city's water springs. So, Elisha asked the men for a bowl of salt. "From now on, this water will be fresh and pure," said Elisha.

MAY 21

A WIDOW CAME TO SEE Elisha. "Before my husband died, he borrowed some money," she said. "The man who loaned it wants me to pay him back. He will take my two sons as his slaves if I don't. Please help me, because I have no money!" Elisha thought hard. "Do you have anything at all?" he asked. "Just one small jug of oil," the woman replied. "Get as many jars as you can, then pour your oil into them," said Elisha.

The woman's oil didn't run out until the last jar was full.

"Sell all this oil," Elisha told her. "Then pay off your debt. You will never be poor again."

MAY 22

ELISHA WAS ALWAYS

traveling around the country, teaching and helping God's people. Whenever he visited a place called Shunem, a local farmer's wife invited him to stay at their house. She even had a guest room built for him. Elisha wanted to do something to repay the woman for her kindness. Although she was rich, there was one thing her money couldn't buy. She desperately wanted a child. Elisha called the woman to his room. "This time next year, you will be holding a baby son in your arms," he said. The woman could not believe what she had heard, because she had been married many years. But, one year later, Elisha's words came true.

MAY 23

THE FARMER and his wife adored their son. One day, the little boy was with his father in the fields when he cried out in pain. The farmer sent him home, and his wife nursed him. But he died a few hours later. The woman carried her dead son up to Elisha's room. Then she left the house to find Elisha and tell him what had happened. Elisha returned with her to see the dead child for himself. The prophet went into the boy's room and prayed. Suddenly, a sneeze broke the silence – then another, and another. The boy sneezed seven times, opened his eyes, and sat up in bed. His parents wept for joy.

153

MAY 24

GOD TOLD ELISHA that Israel was about to suffer a terrible famine. Elisha became worried about the farmer's wife and her family in Shunem. "Go and find somewhere else to live," he warned them. So they packed up their belongings and traveled to another country, where they set up home.

When the famine was over, the family returned to find that strangers had taken over their land. The mother went to the king for help. By coincidence, the king was listening to stories of Elisha's miracles and had just heard how Elisha had brought her son back to life. "Give this woman everything that belongs to her," ordered the king.

MAY 25

NAAMAN was a successful officer in the Aramean army. Unfortunately, he suffered from a nasty skin disease. One day, his slave girl made a suggestion. "There is a prophet in my homeland who could heal you," she said. "His name is Elisha." So, Naaman traveled to Israel to find Elisha. The prophet told Naaman to wash seven times in the Jordan River. At first Naaman refused. "Have I come all this way to jump into a dirty river?" he moaned. But his servant persuaded him to obey Elisha. When Naaman bathed in the river, his skin became smooth again.

He ran to thank Elisha. "Now I know that the God of Israel is the true God," he said.

MAY 26

ARAM AND ISRAEL were at war, and things were going badly for the Aramean army. "A spy is giving away our secrets," said the king of Aram. His officers suspected Elisha. "This holy man knows everything. He must be helping the king of Israel." So, the king of Aram sent his army to capture Elisha. Soldiers surrounded the city where Elisha was staying. When Elisha saw that they were about to attack, he prayed to God to make them blind. Then he led the blind soldiers to his king, where God restored their sight. "Shall I kill them?" asked the king. "No," said Elisha. "Feed them, then send them home." After this, there were no more attacks by Aram on Israel.

MAY 27

QUEEN ATHALIAH OF JUDAH was a cruel and evil woman. When her son, King Ahaziah, died, she murdered all her grandchildren and seized the throne for herself. But her baby grandson Joash survived. His nurse hid him in the temple of God, where he lived in secret for six years. When Joash was seven years old, the people had had enough of his evil grandmother. When they found out that Joash was still alive, they crowned him king and killed Athaliah. Joash grew up to love God, and he encouraged his people to do the same. The temple had been damaged during his grandmother's reign, and he made sure it was properly repaired.

MAY 28

GOD WAS NOT HAPPY

with the people of Nineveh city.
They had turned away from
him and were living bad,
sinful lives. Jonah was
one of God's special
messengers. God told
Jonah to go to Nineveh and tell
the people to change their ways,
or they would be punished. Jonah did
not want to do as God asked. Instead, he ran away,
trying to hide from God. He set off for the port
of Joppa, where he got on a boat bound for
Tarshish. This was about as far away from the
city of Nineveh as Jonah could hope to get.
Tired out from his travels, Jonah went
below deck and fell into a deep sleep.

MAY 29

NOT LONG AFTER the boat had set sail, God sent a big storm. Towering waves rocked the boat, making the sailors afraid for their lives. They woke Jonah and cast lots to see who was to blame for the danger. Jonah's name came up.

"I have sinned against God by trying to run away from him," admitted Jonah. "Throw me overboard." The sailors did so, and immediately the storm stopped.

MAY 30

G OD DID NOT LET Jonah drown in the sea. Instead, he sent a big fish to swallow Jonah whole! Jonah spent three days and three nights inside the fish. He had plenty of time to think about how he had behaved, and now he was sorry for disobeying God. Jonah thanked God for saving him. "From now on, I'll do whatever you ask," said Jonah. So, God told the fish to swim close to land and spit Jonah out onto the shore. "Go to Nineveh," said God.

MAY 31

WHEN JONAH ARRIVED in Nineveh, he told the people to say sorry for their sins. The people did so, and God forgave them. Jonah thought that God should have made the people suffer more. He sat and sulked under the shade of a vine. God sent a worm to nibble the vine's roots. The vine withered and died, and Jonah's shade disappeared. "I'm so hot and upset I want to die!" moaned Jonah. "You're angry because this plant is dead, but you did nothing to look after it," said God. "I care for the people of Nineveh and don't want them to suffer and die."

161

JUNE 1

KING JOASH OF JUDAH was a wise ruler. He taught his people to love and obey God. He spent many years restoring the temple in Jerusalem to its former glory. While Joash ruled in Judah, the people followed his good example and turned their backs on false gods. But, the kings of Judah that followed Joash were not good like him. They were mean and evil. The worst one of all was King Ahaz. He sacrificed his own son to false gods, and he stole silver and gold from the temple in Jerusalem. Finally, he closed the temple altogether. Things were looking very bad for the people of Judah.

June 2

THE KINGS OF ISRAEL were even worse than the kings of Judah. They set the people of Israel a terrible example. They worshipped false gods in holy places and disobeyed God's laws. God told them to change their ways, or Israel would be destroyed. But nobody listened. Altars to worthless idols sprang up everywhere, and the people copied the wicked ways of their kings. God's patience finally ran out. At the time King Ahaz was ruling in Judah, God allowed the kingdom of Israel to be destroyed. The king of Assyria conquered Israel. He sent the people of Israel to live in foreign lands, and he brought foreign people to live in Israel.

JUNE 3

AFTER KING AHAZ died, his
son Hezekiah ruled over the land of
Judah. Hezekiah was a good king, unlike
his evil father. King Hezekiah loved God
and was shocked at how his father had
behaved. There were altars to false gods
on every street corner, and the temple
was closed. As soon as Hezekiah became
king, he worked hard to please God.

He sent priests into the damaged
and neglected temple to remove
anything that was sinful in God's
sight. As soon as the temple
was repaired and purified,
King Hezekiah dedicated the
building to God once more.
There were celebrations
in Jerusalem when
the temple was
reopened.

JUNE 4

DURING THE FESTIVAL of Passover, King Hezekiah wanted as many people as possible to worship God in the reopened temple. At Passover, the people remembered how God had rescued them from slavery in Egypt. Hezekiah sent royal messengers throughout the land, urging God's people to come to Jerusalem for Passover. As a result, huge crowds flocked to the city, and the festival was a great success. By the time the celebrations were over, there were no altars to false gods anywhere in Jerusalem. Then the people traveled all over Judah, destroying any idols they found.

165

JUNE 5

HEZEKIAH ALWAYS put God first. For this reason, God blessed him and he was a successful king. But, times were not always easy for Hezekiah. The king of Assyria invaded Judah, and God's people were very frightened. "I will turn Jerusalem into a strong fortress," said Hezekiah. He ordered broken parts of the city wall to be repaired and watchtowers to be built around the city defenses. Then he told his army officials to block off all the springs and rivers around Jerusalem. "Why should the Assyrian soldiers find water to drink?" said Hezekiah. Finally, the defenses were in place, and the people of Jerusalem waited for their enemies.

JUNE 6

HEZEKIAH SPOKE to the people. "Be brave!" he said. "The king of Assyria may have a huge army, but we are stronger than him because God is on our side." Soon afterward, the Assyrians arrived. Their king sent a message to frighten Hezekiah. "What makes you think your God will rescue you?" he said. "None of our enemies has ever been saved before." Hezekiah did not answer, but he prayed to God for help. God sent an angel who destroyed the Assyrian army, and the king of Assyria was forced to return home in disgrace. People from all over Judah brought gifts to Jerusalem to thank God for his help.

JUNE 7

THE TWO KINGS who followed Hezekiah were bad kings. They turned away from God and worshipped idols. Josiah was very young when he became king, but he loved God. He pulled down the altars to false gods and repaired the temple in Jerusalem. While this repair work

was going on in the temple, a priest named Hilkiah made a very important find. He came across the long lost Book of the Law, containing the commandments that God had given to Moses many years before. King Josiah became very sad when the laws were read out to him. "God will punish us, because we have disobeyed him," said the king.

JUNE 8

HILKIAH THE PRIEST and some court officials went to see a prophetess named Huldah. The king wanted to hear what she had to say about the Book of the Law. Huldah told the men to give King Josiah a solemn message. "God says he will punish the people for disobeying him," said Huldah. "He will bring down disaster on the kingdom of Judah!" Huldah then added a few words of comfort. "But tell your king that God has seen how sorry he is for the people's disobedience. God will not punish them until after Josiah's death."

JUNE 9

THE KING'S MEN listened to Huldah the prophetess, then went to tell Josiah what she had said. Right away, the king summoned the people to a big meeting at the temple in Jerusalem. Everyone was invited, from the least important citizens to the most powerful officials. Josiah stood up and read the whole Book of the Law to the crowd. Then he made a vow before the people, promising to keep God's laws with all his heart and soul. "Each one of you must also promise to follow God," he told them.

From that day on, and for the rest of Josiah's reign, the people of Judah obeyed God.

JUNE 10

JEREMIAH WAS TRAINING to be a priest while King Josiah was still a young man. One day, Jeremiah heard God speak to him. "I have chosen you to be my special messenger," said God. "I want you to pass on my words to the people." Jeremiah was nervous. "But I'm just a child!" he stammered. "Do not be afraid," replied God. He reached out and touched Jeremiah's lips. "I will put words into your mouth," God told him. God knew his people did not love him. He told Jeremiah that the kingdom of Judah would be destroyed. "You must warn my people," said God.

171

JUNE 11

FROM THAT DAY ON, Jeremiah warned the people to change their wicked ways, or God would destroy Judah. Despite these warnings, no one listened to the prophet. One day, when Jehoiakim was king of Judah, God told Jeremiah to write down all the holy messages he had ever been given. "If you read them out to the people, perhaps they will be sorry," said God. Jeremiah's list was read aloud in the temple and also to King Jehoiakim in his palace. The king became angry as he listened. Instead of asking for forgiveness, he cut up Jeremiah's writings and threw them into the fire. Jeremiah was not discouraged. He just wrote down another list for the people to read.

JUNE 12

MANY YEARS LATER, when King Zedekiah ruled over Judah, the city of Jerusalem was attacked once again. This time, the enemy was the powerful king of Babylon. Fierce battles were raging all around Jerusalem. God spoke to the prophet Jeremiah. "Go and speak to Zedekiah. Tell him that I am about to hand this city over to the king of Babylon, who will burn it to the ground. Zedekiah will be taken prisoner. But I promise that Zedekiah will not be killed. He will die a peaceful death and be buried with honor." Jeremiah went to see his king and gave him God's message.

JUNE 13

KING ZEDEKIAH and the people of Jerusalem did not want to listen to Jeremiah's gloomy predictions. They preferred to ignore him, even though the king of Babylon and his army had surrounded the city. One day Jeremiah was arrested by some of the king's men. "You're upsetting our soldiers," they said. His accusers threw him down a deep well to keep him quiet. There was no water in the well, only thick mud, and Jeremiah sank down in the mud. But, a palace official named Ebed-melech heard what had happened and went to see the king. "Set Jeremiah free, or he will starve to death," he pleaded. The king agreed, and so Jeremiah was lifted out of the well.

JUNE 14

THE PROPHET Ezekiel was another prophet who warned God's people about the destruction of Judah. One day, he saw a dark storm cloud in the sky. In the middle was a brightly shining object. As Ezekiel watched, the dazzling object broke away from the cloud and rushed toward him. It was like a huge, living machine, with wheels to move fast on land and wings to fly through the air. Four beasts, each with a different face, made up the creature. Right at the heart of the strange being glowed a ball of fire. Ezekiel bowed to the ground, because he knew he was in the presence of God.

JUNE 15

GOD WANTED HIS PEOPLE to understand that Jerusalem was doomed. He told Ezekiel to act out what the future held. So the prophet carved a picture of Jerusalem on a brick, then used soil to form a barricade around the brick. He put a tin plate between himself and the brick, like a wall. All this was to show how the people of Jerusalem were going to be attacked and trapped in their city. Ezekiel baked a small loaf of bread each day, which he ate with two small cupfuls of water. Soon, the people of Jerusalem would have to ration their food and water in the same way.

JUNE 16

EVERYTHING THAT Jeremiah and Ezekiel had warned about took place. The people of Jerusalem were starving when the king of Babylon and his army finally smashed through the walls to take the city. The attackers set fire to the king's palace and the houses of the people.

Then they burned down the temple and stole all its treasures. Many of the people were killed, and those that remained were carried off to Babylon as slaves. King Zedekiah tried to escape, but he was captured. Zedekiah watched helplessly as the soldiers killed his sons, then he was blinded and taken in chains to Babylon.

JUNE 17

GOD'S PEOPLE were very sad living as prisoners in Babylon, hundreds of miles away from home. These exiles from Judah became known as Jews. They never forgot they were God's people, and they had plenty of time to feel sorry for their mistakes. Above all, they longed to be back in Jerusalem. One song that was written about this difficult time is a reminder of the suffering God's people went through. "We sit down by the rivers of Babylon and weep when we remember Jerusalem," sang God's people. "How can we sing songs to the Lord while we are living in a strange land?"

JUNE 18

EZEKIEL TOLD THE PEOPLE that God had come to him in a dream. "I was in a valley littered with hundreds of human bones," said Ezekiel. "God told me that he was going to bring all these dry bones back to life. Suddenly, I saw the bones join together to form skeletons. Flesh began to cover the skeletons, and soon the valley was filled with human bodies. 'Tell the winds to breathe life into these corpses,' God told me. I obeyed, and the dead began to breathe again. 'These are my people,' said God. 'One day I will breathe new life and fresh hope into their broken nation.' "

JUNE 19

JOB WAS A RICH farmer. He had a happy family and lived an honest life. God was pleased with Job, because he was always generous and kind to other people. Satan, the evil enemy of God, was interested in Job. "This man only obeys God because of the good things he is given in return," said Satan. God let Satan put Job to the test. "Take away everything Job loves," God told Satan. "He will still be true to me." So terrible things started happening to Job. All his farm animals were either killed or stolen by raiders. Then a desert storm took the lives of his children. Poor Job was heartbroken.

JUNE 20

DESPITE EVERYTHING, Job refused to blame God for his misfortune. "We are happy when God is good to us, so we must bear it when he sends trouble," he said. Three friends of Job came to give him some advice. "Say sorry to God for your sins," they said. Job knew he had done nothing wrong, but he wanted to ask God why his life had fallen apart. A storm broke, and God spoke to Job. He helped Job to realize that it is trust, not understanding, that is important. Then God rewarded Job by making him twice as wealthy as before and blessing him with ten more children.

JUNE 21

THE KING OF BABYLON

told his servant to pick some young men who had been taken prisoners from Jerusalem. "Take them to my palace to be trained as my advisers," he ordered. A man named Daniel and three of his friends were among the chosen few. When they arrived at the palace, they were given the best royal food. But they refused it, asking instead for simple food that would not conflict with their worship of God. Their master agreed to give them a diet of plain food for ten days. When he saw how healthy they looked, he agreed that they could eat as they wished.

JUNE 22

ONE DAY, the king summoned his advisers. "I have had a strange dream," he said. "Tell me what I dreamed, then explain it to me, or you will die." That night, God told Daniel about the king's dream. The next morning, Daniel spoke to the king. "You dreamed of a statue with a head of gold, chest and arms of silver, belly of bronze, legs of iron, and feet of clay," said Daniel. "Then, a great stone fell on the statue, smashing it to pieces. The king was amazed. "That's right!" he said. "Your empire is the statue's golden head," said Daniel. "After you, other empires will rise, inferior to yours. But one day God will send a king whose kingdom will last forever. This king is the stone you saw in your dream."

183

JUNE 23

THE KING could not forget the big statue in his dream. "Wouldn't it be wonderful to make a real statue, just like the one I dreamed about?" he thought. "But this statue would be the image of me, and I would make it in gold, from head to toe." The king ordered work to start on his statue right away. When it was finished, it was an incredible sight. The gleaming figure stood fifteen times taller than the tallest man. "Now the people must bow down to my statue," commanded the king. "Anyone who refuses will be burned alive!" Everybody knew the king always meant what he said.

JUNE 24

DANIEL'S THREE FRIENDS refused the king's command. "We will not worship a statue," they said. "We must be true to our God." The king was furious. "Throw them into the fire," he shouted. So, Daniel's friends were put into a blazing furnace. It was heated seven times hotter than usual. As the king watched, he saw another person among the flames. The fourth man looked like an angel. The king ordered Daniel's friends to come out of the furnace. They emerged, unharmed by the fire. Mysteriously, the fourth man had disappeared. "Your God has saved you!" the king said. "He is great and must be praised."

185

JUNE 25

THE KING OF BABYLON had another strange dream, this time of a very tall tree. "Cut down this tree," ordered an angel. The tree stump turned into a man. "This man must live like a wild animal," said the angel. "He has to learn that God rules the world." Daniel explained the dream to the king. "You are the tree," he said. "If you don't obey God, you will lose your power." But the king did not obey God, and everything happened as Daniel said. A madness came over the king, and he lived like an animal for many years. When he finally returned to his palace, he never disobeyed God again.

JUNE 26

BELSHAZZAR, the new king of Babylon, held a big banquet for his friends. "Get the golden cups," Belshazzar ordered. He made everyone drink from the holy cups that his father had taken from the temple in Jerusalem. Suddenly, Belshazzar went pale with terror. "I can see a hand, writing on the wall over there!" he cried. The king asked Daniel to tell him what the words meant. "You have disobeyed God, and your empire is about to end," said Daniel. That night, Darius, the king of Persia, attacked Babylon and killed King Belshazzar.

June 27

KING DARIUS was very impressed with Daniel's wisdom, so he made him his chief adviser. But this made some of the palace officials jealous, and they plotted to get rid of Daniel. Soon they had a plan and went to see the new king. "We think that there should be a law against people praying to any other god but you," they said. "If they do, they should be thrown to the lions." The king liked this idea so much, he passed a new law to put it into practice. The jealous officials knew that Daniel prayed to God three times a day. Daniel heard about the new law, but he refused to obey it. He carried on praying three times a day, as usual.

JUNE 28

DANIEL'S ENEMIES were delighted when they caught him breaking the law. They arrested him and took him to the king. Reluctantly, the king had to admit that Daniel had disobeyed him. "Throw him to the lions!" cried the palace officials. King Darius had no choice but to send Daniel to his death. At dawn, the king ran to the lions' den. "Did your God save you?" the king called out. "God sent an angel to protect me, because I have done nothing wrong!" replied Daniel. King Darius was overjoyed that Daniel was safe. Then he ordered Daniel's accusers to be thrown into the den.

JUNE 29

KING XERXES was the powerful ruler of the Persian empire. He was used to having his own way, especially in his own household. One day, he called for his wife, Queen Vashti. She was busy and refused to come. Kind Xerxes was furious and banished her forever from his presence. The king decided to find a new queen, so he rounded up all the suitable young women in the land.

They gathered in the palace for the king to make his choice. Esther was an orphan from a Jewish family. She was gentle and kind, as well as beautiful. As soon as the king saw Esther, he decided to make her his queen.

JUNE 30

ESTHER was excited but also very nervous. She knew that, if she did wrong, she would be punished like Queen Vashti. Esther kept secret the fact that she was a Jew. This was probably good, because the king's chief minister, a man named Haman, hated the Jewish people. Haman hatched an evil plot to murder every Jew in the empire. He went to see King Xerxes. "Your Majesty," he said, "I know of some trouble makers who always disobey your laws. They are the Jews. If you let me set a date to kill them all, I promise you a vast sum of money." The king agreed to this wicked plan.

JULY 1

ESTHER'S COUSIN Mordecai worked at the palace. When he heard about Haman's plot, he sent a message to Esther. "Beg the king to save the lives of the Jewish people," he urged. Esther knew this would be a dangerous thing to do. She sent word back to her cousin. "It is against the law to go to the king uninvited," she said. "The punishment is death!" "If you don't go, you will die anyway, because you are a Jew," replied Mordecai. "Perhaps it was God's will for you to become queen, so you could rescue his people." So Esther pushed aside her fears and went to visit the king.

JULY 2

TO ESTHER'S GREAT RELIEF King Xerxes was pleased to see her. "What can I do for you?" he asked. "I would like to invite you and Haman to a banquet," replied Esther nervously. Haman was delighted to be invited. He felt more important than ever. While they were eating, Esther finally dared to speak out. "There is a man who is plotting to kill my family and all my people," she said quietly. "Who is this scoundrel?" asked the king. Esther pointed across the table at Haman. The king exploded with rage. "He shall pay for this with his own life!" he cried. Esther had saved her people from a terrible tragedy.

JULY 3

FOR MANY YEARS, God's people were forced to stay in Babylon. During the rule of King Cyrus of Persia, things began to improve at last. God told King Cyrus to let his people go back to Jerusalem. So, the king made an announcement to everyone in his empire. "God has commanded me to rebuild the temple in Jerusalem," he proclaimed. "The Jewish people may now return home. Those who are able should give what they can to the temple funds." King Cyrus did everything in his power to help with the work. He made sure that all the precious things that had been stolen from God's temple were taken back to Jerusalem.

JULY 4

WITH HAPPY HEARTS, God's people finally returned home. The time came to dedicate the new temple site to God. Huge crowds of people gathered in the city of Jerusalem. Everyone watched as the priests built an altar and offered sacrifices to God. Then the building work began. Once the foundation stones were laid, the people danced and sang for joy. But, many foreigners had settled in Judah. These people did not approve of the plans to rebuild the temple and the ruined city of Jerusalem. They did their best to stop the work.

JULY 5

ONCE THE TEMPLE had been rebuilt, it was clear that the people needed a new leader. God chose Ezra, a good and wise teacher. Ezra had studied the writings of Moses and always tried to obey God's law. God was pleased with Ezra and rewarded him with success. King Artaxerxes, the powerful ruler of the Persian empire, gave Ezra everything he asked for when he left Babylon for Jerusalem. The king sent Ezra to the Jewish capital with a letter addressed to the people, ordering them to be generous and to help Ezra in his work.

JULY 6

THERE WAS STILL a lot of work to be done in Jerusalem. Even though the temple had been repaired, most of the city still lay in ruins. The fortress walls were broken down, and a fire had destroyed the city gates. Jerusalem was open to attack at any time. News of this state of affairs traveled back to the palace of King Artaxerxes. One of the king's chief servants, Nehemiah, had stayed behind in Babylon when God's people had returned home. Nehemiah was very sad when he heard how grim things were in Jerusalem. He prayed to God. "Please help me return to Jerusalem to rebuild your city."

JULY 7

NEHEMIAH WAS ONE of the king's most trusted servants, and he knew it would not be easy to leave the royal court. But he desperately wanted to help repair Jerusalem's shameful damage. One day, King Artaxerxes noticed Nehemiah's troubled expression. "What is wrong?" he asked. "You are not ill, so something must have upset you." Nehemiah did not want to anger the king, but he had to take this chance to speak. He prayed for courage. Then Nehemiah told the king what was on his mind. "Would you allow me to go back home to help rebuild Jerusalem?" To Nehemiah's great relief, the king agreed to his request.

JULY 8

THE KING DID EVERYTHING he could to help Nehemiah. He packed his loyal servant off with a special travel pass and a royal guard for his protection. The king also gave permission for Nehemiah to use timber from the royal forest to help with the building work.

When Nehemiah first arrived in Jerusalem, he did not tell anyone about his plans for the city. Instead, he went out alone in the middle of the night, to explore the city and to see what needed to be done. Nehemiah was shocked when he saw how much damage there was. It was obvious that urgent work had to begin right away.

JULY 9

THE MORNING AFTER his secret inspection of Jerusalem, Nehemiah called together the leaders of the people for a meeting. "Jerusalem was once a great and powerful city. We are in disgrace because it is now no more than a pile of rubble!" he said. "Let's rebuild our city and restore our pride!" Nehemiah's enthusiasm was infectious, and the people got to work. There were many enemies of God's people. They wanted Jerusalem to stay as it was, weak and defenseless. But no matter how much they bullied and jeered, the rebuilding continued. When they threatened to attack, God's people simply armed themselves and kept on working.

JULY 10

LIFE WAS NOT EASY for God's people when they returned home. Some families had lost their farms and all their possessions. The people came to Nehemiah with their problems. "We cannot afford to buy food," they complained. "Some of us have even had to sell our children as slaves because we are so poor." Nehemiah realized that the powerful leaders in Jerusalem were to blame. They had raised taxes so much that the ordinary people were being forced to live in misery. Nehemiah ordered the leaders to give back everything they had taken from the people. From then on, he made sure this terrible situation never happened again.

JULY 11

GOD'S PEOPLE WORKED very hard to repair the walls that surrounded Jerusalem. Nehemiah organized the volunteers into groups, so that different sections of the city defenses could be rebuilt at the same time. Sometimes all the members of a family would work on a part of the wall close to their home. Teams of priests tackled some stretches of the wall, and people who shared the same trade, such as goldsmiths, also teamed up to work together. Each day, work began at sunrise and continued until nightfall. Everyone realized how important it was to make Jerusalem a safe place to live.

JULY 12

THE ENEMIES OF GOD'S PEOPLE

did everything in their power to stop the building work, but all their efforts failed. The determination and hard work of the people paid off, and the city walls were finished at last. It was time to celebrate. Priests poured into Jerusalem from all the surrounding towns and villages.

The city walls were dedicated to God, then the people began to dance to the music of harps and cymbals. The leaders of the people marched around the top of the new city walls, while two choirs sang praises to God.

July 13

THROUGHOUT THEIR TROUBLED

history, the Jews had always looked forward to a time when God would send a special king to save his people. This longed-for king was known as the "Messiah." Many years before, the prophet Isaiah spoke about a child who would grow up to be called the "Prince of Peace." His reign would bring freedom to God's people.

At long last, the time came for God to make Isaiah's words come true. Things did not happen in the way many expected. God came down to earth as a baby, born into an ordinary family in the humblest of surroundings.

JULY 14

MARY LIVED IN NAZARETH, a small town in Galilee. She was engaged to marry Joseph, a local carpenter. One day, God sent the angel Gabriel to visit Mary. The angel told Mary that she was going to have a very special baby boy. This baby would be the Son of God. "You will give him the name Jesus," said Gabriel. Mary listened quietly. "How can all this be?" she asked. "God's Holy Spirit will make it happen," said the angel. "Nothing is impossible for God." Mary was amazed and delighted at what the angel had told her.

JULY 15

ZECHARIAH was a priest. He and his wife Elizabeth were sad because they did not have any children, and now they were too old. One day, Zechariah was inside the temple when the angel Gabriel came to him. "Your wife will have a baby son," said Gabriel, "and you shall call him John." Zechariah was very surprised by this news. "How can I be sure this is true?" he asked. Gabriel told him that because he had not believed God's message, he would not be able to speak until the baby was born. Then the angel left, and Zechariah found that he was unable to talk. Soon, he found out that Elizabeth was indeed expecting a child.

JULY 16

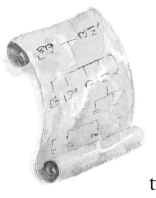

JOSEPH THE CARPENTER

was a kind man and came from a very good family. He could trace his family tree all the way back to King David, and he was proud of this. Joseph wanted to marry Mary, but he was sad when he found out she was going to have a baby. Then, one night, Joseph had a dream. In the dream, God told Joseph not to worry, but to go ahead and marry Mary. Her baby was going to be born because of the special power of God's Holy Spirit. God wanted Joseph to take care of Mary and her new baby.

JULY 17

MARY WENT TO VISIT ELIZABETH, who was her relative. Elizabeth was also expecting a special baby and was very happy about it. Mary knew she would be able to talk to Elizabeth about the wonderful things that the angel Gabriel had told her. When Mary arrived at the house, Elizabeth ran out to meet her. The two women hugged with joy, and Mary sang a song of thanks to God. Mary stayed with Elizabeth for a few months, then returned to Nazareth.

JULY 18

ELIZABETH GAVE BIRTH to a baby son, just as the angel had said. When the time came to name the child, their friends and relatives expected them to name him Zechariah, after his father. "Our son is to be called John," said Elizabeth. "But nobody in our family has that name," said their relatives. Zechariah still could not speak, so they brought him a writing tablet to find out what he thought. "His name is John," he wrote. Suddenly, Zechariah was able to speak again. He began to sing for joy, praising God for his goodness.

JULY 19

AT ABOUT THE TIME that Mary's baby was due, the Roman emperor, Augustus, ordered all his people to return to their home towns. This was because he wanted to count every citizen in his empire. So Joseph and Mary left their house in Nazareth and traveled to Bethlehem. This small town was the place where Joseph's ancestor King David had been born. The journey to Bethlehem was uncomfortable, especially for Mary, who was to give birth soon.

JULY 20

MARY AND JOSEPH

arrived in Bethlehem after a long, hot journey. Darkness was falling, and they were both exhausted. They needed to find a place to stay for the night. But everywhere they tried was full of travelers like themselves. Finally, a kind innkeeper took pity on them. He had no spare room to offer, but said they could sleep in the stable where he kept his animals. It was here, later that night, that Mary gave birth to her baby son and named him Jesus, as God had said. She wrapped him up in cloths and laid him in a manger.

JULY 21

THAT SAME NIGHT, some shepherds were guarding their sheep outside Bethlehem. Suddenly, the dark sky lit up with a dazzling light, and an angel appeared. "I bring you good news!" said the angel. "Tonight something wonderful has happened. The Son of God has been born! Go to Bethlehem, and you will find him wrapped in cloths and lying in a manger."

JULY 22

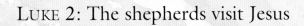

THE WHOLE SKY was soon filled with hundreds of angels, singing songs of joyful praise to God. The shepherds were amazed by this incredible sight. When the angels left, the men discussed what to do. They agreed to go at once to find the baby the angels had told them about. So, they left their sheep and set off toward the nearby town of Bethlehem. It was not long before the shepherds found Mary and Joseph in a stable, with baby Jesus lying in a manger. Everything was just as the angel had said it would be. Silently and joyfully, the shepherds knelt down to worship the baby.

JULY 23

THE SHEPHERDS told Mary what the angel had said about her son, and she treasured their words in her heart. After a while, the shepherds left the stable to return to their fields. They were all full of wonder at what they had seen that night. As they went on their way, the shepherds could not keep quiet. They ran through the streets of Bethlehem, singing and praising God. From that time on, they told everyone they met about the baby Jesus.

JULY 24

MARY AND JOSEPH WERE PROUD

of their baby boy. They were eager to bring him up in the traditions of the Jewish faith. One of the first duties they faced was to give their new son a name. Jewish babies were named when they were eight days old. Mary and Joseph held a special naming ceremony, when they told everybody that they were going to call their baby "Jesus." This was the name that the angel Gabriel had told Mary to give her baby, when he brought her the joyful news that she was to be mother of God's only son.

215

JULY 25

WHEN JESUS was a few months old, Mary and Joseph took him to the temple in Jerusalem. There they met an old man named Simeon, who had been true to God all his life. As soon as Simeon saw baby Jesus, he took him in his arms. Mary and Joseph were amazed at what Simeon had to say. "God told me I would see the Savior of the World before I died," said the old man. "Now I have seen the Lord, and I can die a happy man."

JULY 26

THERE WAS AN OLD LADY who was also in the temple when Mary and Joseph arrived with Jesus. Her name was Anna, and she was eighty-four years old. She spent all her time in the temple praying to God and singing songs of praise. When Anna caught sight of baby Jesus, she knew just how special he was. She hurried over to Mary and Joseph and knelt down before their son, thanking God for his goodness.

From that day on, Anna told everyone she met in the temple that God's promised Messiah had come.

JULY 27

SOME WISE MEN FROM THE EAST saw a bright star in the night sky. This star meant that an important king had been born. So, they traveled to Jerusalem, hoping to find the new king in this big city. Instead, they met King Herod, who was very jealous of anyone who might try to take his power away. He sent the wise men to Bethlehem because this was where the scriptures said the Messiah would be born. "When you find the king, tell me where he is, so I can worship him too," said Herod. But, secretly, he planned to kill the little baby.

JULY 28

THE WISE MEN LEFT JERUSALEM with the bright star shining above them. They followed the star until it stopped over a small house in Bethlehem. When the wise men entered the house, they saw Mary with her son. They knelt down and offered Jesus special presents.

One gave gold, a gift for a king. Another gave frankincense, for worship in the temple. And another gave myrrh, a spice used in burying the dead. That night, God spoke to the wise men in a dream, warning them not to return to Jerusalem. So, the next day, they set off for home by another route.

JULY 29

BABY JESUS was not safe. King Herod soon realized that the wise men had gone home without telling him where to find the new king. He was furious and gave an order for all the baby boys in Bethlehem to be killed. Joseph had a dream, in which God warned him to leave Bethlehem right away. That same night, Mary and Joseph escaped with Jesus to Egypt. Not long afterward, King Herod died. Only then was it safe for Joseph and his family to return to Israel. So, Jesus and his parents went home to live in Nazareth.

JULY 30

EVERY YEAR, Mary and Joseph traveled to Jerusalem for the festival of Passover. When Jesus was twelve years old, he went along with his parents. When the celebrations were over, Mary and Joseph set off for home. Jerusalem was so crowded that they did not realize that they had left Jesus behind. But soon they noticed he was missing. They searched the city and found him at last in the temple, talking with the Jewish teachers. "Didn't you know I would be in my Father's house?" Jesus asked. He just wanted to be with God, his Father.

JULY 31

GOD WAS ALWAYS with John, from the moment he was born. His parents, Zechariah and Elizabeth, brought him up to live a simple life. He spent most of his time praying. When John was older, he went to live in the desert. He wore rough clothes, and he ate locusts and honey. God gave John an important message to preach.

"You must say sorry to God for the wrong things that you do," John said. "Start all over again and live good, holy lives, because God is going to punish those who don't." Many people were truly sorry for their sins, and John baptized them in the Jordan River to show that God had forgiven them. He became known as John the Baptist.

AUGUST 1

LARGE CROWDS came to hear John preaching in the desert. Some people began to wonder whether John was really the Savior that God had promised. "I am not the Son of God," explained John, "but I am preparing the way for him." One day, Jesus came to see John and asked to be baptized in the river. When Jesus came out of the water, an amazing thing happened. God's Holy Spirit came down and rested on Jesus like a dove. God spoke from heaven, saying to Jesus, "You are my dear Son. I love you, and I am very pleased with you."

AUGUST 2

BEFORE JESUS BEGAN God's work, he went into the desert. He spent forty days and forty nights praying to God. He ate nothing and was hungry.

The Devil tried to tempt Jesus to turn rocks into bread, but Jesus would not use God's power to help himself. Then the Devil promised Jesus all the kingdoms of the world. "Just worship me instead of God," he said. Jesus refused to turn away from God. Finally, the Devil told Jesus to jump from the top of the temple. "Your God will save you!" he said. "I will not put God to the test," replied Jesus. At last, the Devil left Jesus alone.

AUGUST 3

WHEN JESUS LEFT the desert, he began teaching the people about God. He went from town to town, and everyone who heard him thought he was an excellent preacher. Jesus returned to Nazareth, his home town. He taught in the synagogue, where the local people came to pray to God. Some of the people recognized him. "Isn't that Joseph's son?" they asked. He told them that he was the Savior that the prophets had written about.

When they heard this, they drove him out of town and tried to push him off a cliff. But God protected Jesus, and he went safely on his way.

225

AUGUST 4

WHEN JOHN THE BAPTIST first saw Jesus, he knew immediately who he was. "This man is the Son of God," John told his disciples. Two of them followed Jesus and spent the day with him. That evening, one of the men, Andrew, went to find his brother. "Simon, we have found the Savior!" cried Andrew. When Jesus saw Simon, he told him, "From now on your name will be Peter, which means 'rock.' One day, you will be as strong and solid as a rock."

AUGUST 5

THE NEXT DAY, Jesus chose two more of his disciples. He met a man named Philip and asked him to join him on his travels from town to town. Philip went to see his friend Nathaniel. "I have seen the man that Moses and the prophets wrote about in the scriptures," said Philip. "His name is Jesus. He comes from Nazareth." Nathaniel rolled his eyes. "Can anything good come from that town?" he asked. "Come and see," said Philip. So Nathaniel met Jesus, and his doubts disappeared when he heard Jesus speak. "Teacher, you are indeed God's Son, the longed-for Messiah," he said.

227

AUGUST 6

ONE DAY, Jesus and his disciples went to a wedding in the village of Cana. Mary, Jesus' mother, was also a guest. The celebrations were going well, but then the wine ran out. Mary asked Jesus to help. Jesus pointed to some large stone jars. "Pour water into those jars," he told the servants. "Then fill the people's cups from them." The servants did as Jesus had asked. They found that the water turned to wine as they poured it out for the guests. This was Jesus' first miracle.

AUGUST 7

MANY JEWISH LEADERS did not believe that Jesus was the Messiah. But one, named Nicodemus, heard about the amazing things that Jesus was doing, and his curiosity grew. So, he went to meet Jesus at night, because he could not be seen in public with him. "What must I do to enter the Kingdom of Heaven?" asked Nicodemus. "You must be born again," said Jesus. "How can I be born when I'm old?" asked Nicodemus. "When you came into this world as a baby, you were born in the flesh. Now you must be born again in the spirit," said Jesus. "God wants everyone to go to heaven. He sent me into the world to show people the way."

AUGUST 8

JESUS WAS TRAVELING

through Samaria with his disciples. It was hot, and they were thirsty. They came to a well, and Jesus stopped to rest. The disciples walked on to a nearby town to buy some food. Soon, a local woman came to the well to get some water. "May I have a drink?" Jesus asked her. She was very surprised that a Jewish man should speak to her. The Jews looked down on the Samaritans. "If you knew who I was," said Jesus, "it would be you asking *me* for a drink. If you drink the water I can offer, you will never be thirsty again."

AUGUST 9

THE WOMAN SMILED at Jesus. "Where is this wonderful water?" she asked. Jesus explained that God had sent him into the world to offer people the water of everlasting life. "It is a special water. It will refresh your soul," said Jesus. "Go and tell your husband." The woman looked down at her feet. "I have no husband," she muttered. "I know," said Jesus. Then he told her everything there was to know about her life. Astonished, the woman ran to tell her friends. "I have seen the Savior!" she exclaimed. "He has come to offer us everlasting life." They followed her back to the well to meet Jesus. He told them that God loved all the people in the world, Jews and Samaritans alike.

AUGUST 10

JESUS WAS TEACHING a big crowd by Lake Galilee. He borrowed Peter's boat, so that he could be seen and heard by all the people on the shore. When Jesus finished speaking, he asked Peter to throw his nets overboard. "We've been out fishing all night, but didn't catch a thing," said Peter. But, even so, he did as Jesus asked. To his amazement, the nets filled with so many fish that they began to break. Peter knelt down before Jesus.

"I am just a sinful man," he said. "But you are the Lord."

AUGUST 11

MATTHEW WAS NOT VERY POPULAR

because he collected taxes for the hated Romans. One day, Jesus visited Matthew and said to him, "Follow me." Nobody had ever showed such an interest in Matthew before. He left everything to follow Jesus. Matthew was so happy, he held a party for Jesus and invited his friends. When the Jewish teachers saw Jesus at the party, they were shocked. "Why are you friends with sinners?" they asked.

"I have come to help anyone who needs me," said Jesus. "It is easier to help sinners than people who think they are good."

233

AUGUST 12

JESUS WAS STAYING

in Capernaum in Galilee. One day, he preached in the town synagogue. It was full because everyone had come to hear Jesus talk about God.

But there was a man in the crowd who could not listen quietly. An evil spirit took control of him, and he leaped up. "What do you want with us, Jesus?" he shouted. "Have you come to destroy us? I know you are God's Holy One!" Jesus ordered the evil spirit to come out of the man at once. With a loud scream, the man threw himself down before Jesus and the demon left him. The people were amazed at what they had seen.

AUGUST 13

JESUS CHOSE TWELVE of his followers to be his special disciples. He prayed to God to help him make his choice. The twelve he chose were Peter, Andrew, John, Philip, Bartholomew, Matthew, Thomas, Simon, two men named James, and two men named Judas. All Jesus' disciples were ordinary men. Andrew, Peter, John, and his brother James were all fishermen. Jesus told them that they would be "fishers of men." From now on, they would follow Jesus and learn from him. Their main job would be to teach the word of God to as many people as possible.

AUGUST 14

JESUS MET A MAN while he was out walking.
When the man saw Jesus, he fell down at Jesus' feet.
The man was suffering from a terrible skin disease called
leprosy. He had heard about Jesus and believed in him.
"I know you can make me better if you want to," he said,
hiding his face. Jesus reached out and touched the man.
"Be clean!" he said. With that, the man was healed.
Jesus told him not to tell anyone, but news of Jesus'
wonderful powers spread quickly.
Soon, large crowds followed
Jesus everywhere he went.

AUGUST 15

ONE DAY, some men brought their friend to Jesus. He could not walk, so they carried him on a stretcher. The men believed Jesus would heal their friend. Jesus was preaching in a house, but there were so many people there that it was impossible to get near him. So the men thought of a way of reaching Jesus. They climbed onto the roof of the house and made a large hole. Then they lowered their friend down to Jesus. When Jesus saw the men's faith, he said to their friend, "Your sins are forgiven." To prove he had the power to forgive sins, Jesus told the man to get up. The man leaped to his feet and ran home, singing thanks to God.

AUGUST 16

IN JERUSALEM there was a pool of healing waters. A man who had been unable to walk for thirty-eight years was lying beside the pool. Jesus began talking to this man. "Do you really want to get well?" he asked. The man explained that no one would help him into the pool, even though he was desperate to be healed. "Then get up now!" said Jesus. "Pick up your mat and walk!" The man was amazed to find that he could do just as Jesus asked. Some of the Jewish leaders were angry when they heard what Jesus had done. They accused him of breaking the law, because it was the Sabbath, their day of rest.

AUGUST 17

EARLY ONE EVENING, Jesus and his disciples went down to Lake Galilee. The disciples got into a small boat and set off across the water, heading for the lakeside town of Capernaum. As they rowed, dark storm clouds gathered in the sky. Strong winds whipped up the waves and began to rock the boat. Suddenly, the disciples saw someone walking toward them over the water. "It's Jesus!" they cried out in alarm. "Yes, it is me," said Jesus. "Do not be afraid." The disciples pulled Jesus on board their boat. In an instant, the storm disappeared and they approached the safety of the shore.

AUGUST 18

JESUS TRAVELED through the country with his disciples, performing amazing miracles in God's name. Word spread quickly about Jesus' healing powers. People took their sick friends and relatives to meet Jesus in the hope that he could heal them. One day, a man who could not talk was brought to him. The man had been struck dumb by an evil spirit. Jesus ordered the spirit to leave him, and at once the man could speak again. The crowds were amazed, but the Jewish teachers were suspicious and angry. "It is the Devil who helps this man to drive out demons, not God," they said to each other.

AUGUST 19

THE SABBATH was a special day of the week, when Jews were forbidden to work. One Sabbath, Jesus met a man with a shriveled hand. Some Jewish leaders were watching Jesus to see if they could catch him doing wrong.

"Is it against the law to heal on the Sabbath?" they asked. Jesus answered with another question. "Would you rescue your sheep if it fell into a well on the Sabbath?" There was a silence. "Surely a man is worth more than a sheep!" said Jesus. "So it can't be wrong to do good on the Sabbath." With that, Jesus healed the man. The Jewish leaders were furious and plotted to kill Jesus.

AUGUST 20

MANY PEOPLE HEARD about Jesus and his wonderful power to heal the sick. Big crowds followed Jesus everywhere and listened to him talk about God. Often Jesus surprised people by the things that he said, because they were not what people expected to hear. One day, Jesus was teaching about love. "It's easy to love people who love you," he said. "God expects more than this. You should love your enemies, no matter how horrible they are to you. You should always treat other people in the same way that you want them to treat you."
No one had heard teaching like this before.

August 21

JESUS OFTEN MADE UP STORIES to help people understand what he was saying. He told this story to the crowd. "Once a wise man built his house on a rock. He dug deep foundations to make it strong. His foolish friend built his house without foundations, because this was quicker and easier. But then there was a storm. The house with no foundations was washed away in the flood." Jesus looked straight at the people who were listening to him. "If you hear what I say but don't do what I tell you, then you are living in a house with no foundations," he told them.

AUGUST 22

ONE DAY, some Jewish leaders came up to Jesus. "An important officer in the Roman army wants you to help him," they said.

"He is worried about his servant, who is going to die." They told Jesus that the officer was very good to the Jews. So, Jesus set off for the officer's house. But he was met on the way by some of the officer's friends, who told Jesus not to go to the officer's home. "Our friend feels he is not good enough to have you as a guest. But he believes that, if you give the order, his servant will get better." Jesus was amazed at the officer's faith. The men returned and found that the officer's servant had been healed.

AUGUST 23

JESUS AND HIS FRIENDS were walking toward the town of Nain when they stopped to let a funeral procession go by. A man had died, and his mother was weeping. She was a widow, and now she had just lost her only son. Jesus felt sorry for her. "Don't cry," he said. He went over to the dead man and touched him. Everyone watched to see what would happen.

"Get up, young man!" said Jesus. There was a gasp from the crowd as the man sat up. "A great prophet has appeared among us," they said. The mother wept for joy.

245

AUGUST 24

JOHN THE BAPTIST

had known Jesus all his life. But he wanted to be absolutely sure that Jesus really was the Savior that God had promised the world. He sent his followers to ask Jesus this question. Jesus said to them, "You will have the answer if you think about all the things I have done. I have healed the sick, given sight to the blind, made lame people walk, and brought the dead back to life." When John's friends left, Jesus turned to the people with him and said, "John is a good and great man. God sent him to prepare the way for me."

AUGUST 25

JOHN THE BAPTIST always told the truth, even when it was dangerous to do so. He told King Herod that he should not have married Herodias, his brother's wife. This made the king and queen so angry that they threw John into prison. One night, the queen's daughter, Salome, danced for King Herod at a royal feast. The king was very pleased with her performance, and so he promised her anything she wanted. Queen Herodias told Salome to ask for the head of John the Baptist on a plate. King Herod could not go back on his word, so he gave the order for John to be killed.

AUGUST 26

JESUS WAS AT THE HOME of a Jewish priest named Simon. A woman came to see Jesus asking him to forgive her sins. She washed his feet with her tears and covered them with perfume. Simon knew that the woman led a very sinful life. "How can you let her touch you?" he asked. Jesus replied with a question. "If one man owes five hundred gold coins and his friend owes just fifty, which one will be happiest if their debts are forgotten?" "The one who owes more money," replied Simon. "That's right," said Jesus. "People who have more sins to forgive are more grateful when they are forgiven."

AUGUST 27

JESUS TOLD this story to the people. "A farmer sowed some seeds," he said. "A few fell on a path and were pecked by birds. Some fell on stones and weeds, which stopped the seeds from growing. But some seeds fell onto good soil and grew into healthy plants." Jesus then explained his story. "Some people don't listen to God at all. They are like the seeds on the path. Other people listen to God, but when troubles come they don't put what they hear into practice. They are like the seeds among the stones and weeds. People who listen and learn from God are like seeds that grow in good soil."

AUGUST 28

THE STORIES that Jesus told are often called parables. Jesus told several different parables to describe and explain the Kingdom of Heaven. "Imagine that a man discovers a treasure trove buried in a field," Jesus said to his disciples. "He lets out a whoop of joy, then hides the treasure again and rushes off to sell everything he owns. He spends every penny of his money to buy the field and gain this fabulous fortune." The treasure that Jesus was talking about was the Kingdom of God. He wanted his friends to know that it is something so precious that it is worth giving up everything else to have.

AUGUST 29

JESUS TOLD the disciples another parable. His eyes shone with excitement as he spoke again about the Kingdom of Heaven. "Picture it this way," he said. "Imagine a rich man who has spent his whole life buying and selling fine pearls. One day he comes across a pearl, the likes of which he has never seen before. It is absolutely beautiful, simply perfect in every way. The man knows at once that he has to have this pearl, whatever the cost. He sells everything he has, even the fine clothes he is standing in, to make that perfect pearl his own."

AUGUST 30

JESUS WAS STANDING on the shores of Lake Galilee with his disciples. "Let's cross over to the other side," said Jesus. So they got into a boat and set sail. Jesus was tired, and the gentle rocking of the boat soon sent him to sleep. Suddenly, a storm broke. The waves grew tall, and the boat filled up with water. The disciples were terrified. "Wake up!" they shouted to Jesus. "We are going to drown!" Jesus stood up and told the wind and waves to die down. Instantly the lake grew still. "Did you think I would let you die?" Jesus asked. "Where is your faith?"

AUGUST 31

AS JESUS STEPPED OUT of the boat, a man came running out of some caves. He headed straight toward Jesus, screaming and shouting. The man was filled with evil spirits. "Leave me alone!" he cried. "I know you are the Son of God!" Jesus ordered the demons to come out of the man. Immediately, the evil spirits left the man and went into a nearby herd of pigs. Squealing noisily, the pigs charged into the lake and were drowned. The owners of the pigs were amazed when they saw the wild man sitting calmly with Jesus. The man wanted to leave home and follow Jesus, but Jesus sent him home. "Tell everyone what I have done for you," said Jesus.

September 1

A LARGE CROWD OF PEOPLE were pushing and shoving to get a glimpse of Jesus. Everyone was talking about this teacher with the amazing power to heal the sick. As Jesus made his way through the crowd, he stopped. "Who touched me?" he asked. This was a strange question, because so many people were pressing against him. But then a woman stepped forward. "It was me," she said. "I have been ill for twelve years. I knew that if I just touched your cloak, I would get better. Now I am well again." Jesus smiled and said to her, "You have been healed because of your faith in me."

SEPTEMBER 2

JAIRUS WAS FRANTIC with worry. His little girl was so sick, it looked like she was going to die. So Jairus ran to find Jesus and begged him to save his daughter's life. Jesus followed Jairus back to his house. But, on the way, someone stopped them with the news that the girl had died. "Don't be afraid, Jairus," said Jesus. "If you believe in me, your daughter will be healed." When they entered the house, the dead child was lying on a bed. "Little girl, get up," said Jesus. At once, she sat up and smiled. Overjoyed, the girl's parents hugged their daughter.

255

SEPTEMBER 3

As JESUS WAS WALKING in the town, two blind men called out to him. "Please help us, Lord!" they cried. When Jesus entered a house, they followed him. "Do you really believe that I can heal you?" Jesus asked them. "Yes, Lord," they replied. Then Jesus reached out and touched their eyes. "Your faith has restored your sight," he told them. At once, the men were able to see again. Jesus asked them not to talk about what he had done, but they could not keep quiet about the amazing thing that had happened. They went out and told everyone they met about Jesus.

256

SEPTEMBER 4

JESUS WAS IN THE TEMPLE, watching as people came to offer their gifts to God. Some made a great show of what they were doing, so that everyone around could see how generous they were. The rich were proud to give away large sums of money. Unnoticed by everyone except Jesus, a poor widow came into the temple. She put two small copper coins into the collection box and left. Jesus turned to his disciples. "That woman has given more than anyone else here today," he said. "All these people can well afford what they are giving, but she gave away everything that she had."

257

SEPTEMBER 5

THE TIME CAME FOR JESUS to give his twelve disciples the power to heal the sick. Then he told them to go out into the towns and villages to teach people about the Kingdom of Heaven. "Take nothing with you on your travels – neither money, food, nor spare clothes," Jesus told them. "During your time in a town, stay in the same house. If people do not welcome you, shake the dirt off your feet when you leave, as a sign that you are unhappy with them." So the twelve disciples went out to teach everyone they met about God and to make sick people better again.

SEPTEMBER 6

THE DISCIPLES CAME BACK and told Jesus everything they had done. They tried to spend some time together, but the crowds soon caught up with them. Jesus did not turn the people away; he spoke to them about God and healed those in need. More than five thousand people were there, and they were all hungry! Jesus asked his disciples how much food they had. "Just five loaves and two fishes!" they said. So he thanked God and told his disciples to share out the food. Amazingly, there was enough for everyone.

SEPTEMBER 7

A FOREIGN WOMAN came to Jesus and begged him for help. "My poor daughter is being tormented by evil spirits," she cried. The disciples wanted to send the woman away. "She keeps pestering us," they complained. Jesus spoke to her firmly. "I have come to serve the people of Israel," he said. "Is it right for me to help foreigners like you?" The woman gave a bold answer. "Even dogs eat crumbs that fall from their master's table," she argued. Jesus smiled. "You have great faith! I will do as you ask," he said. And at that very moment, the woman's daughter was healed.

SEPTEMBER 8

JESUS WAS PRAYING one day, while his disciples were sitting nearby. Suddenly, he got up and went to join his friends. "Who do people say that I am?" Jesus asked.

"Some people say you are John the Baptist," they said. "Others think that you are Elijah, or one of the other ancient prophets, come back from the dead." Then he asked another question. "Who do you say that I am?" There was silence as each disciple searched for an answer. Then Peter spoke up. "You are the Messiah that the prophets wrote about, sent by God!" he declared.

SEPTEMBER 9

JESUS TOOK Peter, John, and James up onto a mountain to pray. As Jesus began to pray, the disciples saw that he was changing before their eyes. His face looked different, and his clothes were dazzling like the sun. Jesus was talking to Moses and Elijah, who had been leaders of God's people long ago. Then a cloud came down and covered them all, and a voice said, "This is my Son. You must listen to him." The disciples knew that God had spoken to them.

SEPTEMBER 10

ON THEIR WAY BACK
from the mountain, Jesus and the
three disciples were met by a big
crowd. A man stepped
forward. "Please help
my son," he begged
Jesus. "He is my only
child, and an evil spirit
is making him have terrible fits. I asked your
disciples to heal him, but they could not."
Jesus told the man to bring his son to him.
But, as they were walking toward Jesus,
another fit threw the boy to the ground.
"Leave this boy in peace," said Jesus,
ordering the evil spirit to come out of him.
At once, the boy became well, and Jesus
gave him back to his father. Everyone
there was amazed at what they had seen.

263

SEPTEMBER 11

ONE DAY, THE TWELVE DISCIPLES began to quarrel about which one of them was the greatest. They all believed Jesus would soon become king, and each thought they deserved the best position in his kingdom. Jesus realized they had become too proud. He asked a small boy to come over and join them.

"God does not see greatness in the same way that you do," Jesus said. "Let me tell you this. Unless you change and become like little children, not one of you will enter the Kingdom of Heaven. Whoever humbles himself like this child will be the greatest in that kingdom."

SEPTEMBER 12

ON THE WAY to Jerusalem, Jesus and his disciples met a man who wanted to follow Jesus wherever he went. Jesus told him this would not be easy, because he would have nowhere to call home. Jesus asked another man to come with him. The man said he had to arrange his father's funeral first. "You must put God's work above everything else," Jesus told him. A third man wanted to go with Jesus, but he asked to say goodbye to his family before he left. Jesus knew that the man was unsure about changing his life. "God wants you to look forward, not backward, when you serve him," said Jesus.

SEPTEMBER 13

JESUS TOLD HIS DISCIPLES a parable about forgiveness. "A king ordered one of his servants to give back the money he had borrowed from him. He owed so much that he would have had to sell everything he had to pay back the king. The servant begged for more time to pay. The king took pity on him and agreed to cancel his debt. Soon afterward, the servant met a friend who owed him some money. 'Pay me back,' he demanded 'or I'll have you thrown in jail!' The friend begged for more time, but the servant refused. When the king heard about this, he was furious. 'You should forgive your friend, just as I forgave you,' he said. Then he threw his servant into jail."

SEPTEMBER 14

"A FARMER HIRED some men to work in his vineyard," said Jesus. "He agreed to pay them a silver coin for a day's work. A few hours later, the farmer took on some more workers. In the evening, he employed another group of men. As darkness fell, the farmer gave each worker one silver coin. 'That's not fair!' protested those who had been there all day. 'Did you not agree to the money?' asked the farmer. 'Don't be jealous if I choose to be generous with the others.' " Jesus explained that God loves those who come late to him just as much as those who have always been with him.

SEPTEMBER 15

AN EXPERT IN JEWISH LAW tried to test Jesus. "How can I gain everlasting life?" he asked. "What does the law say?" asked Jesus. "Love God and love your neighbor," he replied. Jesus told him a story to explain what this meant. "A Jewish man was attacked by robbers and left for dead. A priest and another respectable Jew came by, but they didn't stop to help. Then a Samaritan came along, who had never been shown kindness by any Jew. He dressed the man's wounds and gave him the care he needed."

Jesus looked at the expert. "You must show love to everyone you meet, like the good Samaritan," he said.

SEPTEMBER 16

MARY, MARTHA, and their brother Lazarus were friends of Jesus. They lived in the small town of Bethany, which was not far from Jerusalem. Jesus visited them on his way to the city. As soon as Jesus arrived, Mary stopped everything she was doing and sat down to talk to Jesus. Martha, on the other hand, rushed around preparing a meal for their visitor. Before long, Martha became angry with her sister. "Can't you tell her to help me in the kitchen?" she moaned to Jesus. But Jesus shook his head and smiled. "Mary has chosen to spend time with me," he said. "That is the most important thing she can do."

269

SEPTEMBER 17

JESUS WENT OFF by himself to pray. When he had finished, one of his disciples came to talk to him. "We know that John the Baptist taught his disciples to pray," said the disciple. "Could you teach us too?" So Jesus taught them how to pray.

"Begin by praising God and his holy kingdom," said Jesus. Then he told his disciples to think about their own needs. "Pray for your daily bread and ask God to forgive your sins. Then ask God to help you to forgive people who have hurt or upset you. Finally, pray that God will keep you from sinning again."

SEPTEMBER 18

JESUS WANTED his disciples to know that God would answer their prayers. "Imagine your best friend visits you at midnight," said Jesus. "You have no food to offer, so you knock on your neighbor's door and ask for some bread. Your neighbor doesn't really want to help at this late hour. But he gets up and gives you the bread, because you will not stop pestering until he does." Jesus then explained his story. "If a neighbor helps you when you ask, don't you know that God's help is always there. If you ask God for something he will give it to you. It is like knocking on a door that will always be opened to you."

SEPTEMBER 19

ONE DAY A MAN ASKED JESUS for help. "My father has died and my brother won't divide his possessions fairly," he said. "There is more to life than the things you own," said Jesus. Then he told a story. "One harvest, a farmer gathered a huge crop. He decided to build a massive barn to store all the grain. 'Now I'm rich, I can take life easy,' he thought. 'You fool!' said God angrily. 'Tonight your life will end. Can you take any of this with you when you die?' A person is a fool to store up earthly wealth but not have a rich relationship with God," said Jesus.

SEPTEMBER 20

"DO NOT SPEND your time worrying where your next meal will come from, or what you have to wear," Jesus told his disciples. "Life is about much more than food and clothes. Think about the birds. God gives them food to eat, yet you are worth far more to God than birds. Look at the lilies in the fields. God made them more beautiful than the most expensive royal robes – and they are just flowers. If you follow God, he will make sure you have everything you need. Sell your possessions and give the money to the poor. In this way, you will build up treasure in heaven that lasts forever."

273

SEPTEMBER 21

THE SABBATH was the one day
of the week when everybody rested. It was
against the Jewish law to do any work on this
day. One Sabbath, Jesus was in the synagogue
when he met a woman bent over in pain.
She had been unable to stand up straight for
eighteen years. Jesus took pity on the poor
woman and healed her. The leader of the
synagogue was angry. "You should not heal
people on the Sabbath," he told Jesus.

"But you untie your donkey to give
it water on the Sabbath," replied
Jesus. "So why shouldn't I free
this woman from her agony?"
The synagogue leader had no
answer to give.

SEPTEMBER 22

JESUS TOLD this story. "Once there was a very rich man," said Jesus. "Outside his beautiful house lived a poor beggar, named Lazarus. The beggar longed for just one scrap of food from the rich man's table, but he died a hungry man. Lazarus went to live in heaven with Abraham. But when the rich man died, he was thrown into the fires of hell. He called up to Abraham. 'Send Lazarus to warn my brothers about this terrible place!' But Abraham refused. 'Your brothers can read the teachings of the prophets,' he said. 'If they refuse to listen to the prophets, they will not listen to anyone, not even one who has risen from the dead.'"

SEPTEMBER 23

JESUS MET A BEGGAR who had been blind since he was born. "Is this man blind because his parents sinned, or because he did something wrong himself?" asked Jesus' disciples. "Neither he nor his family are to blame," replied Jesus. "This man is blind so that the wonderful power of God can be seen working in his life." With this, Jesus knelt down and spat on the ground. He made some mud from dust and saliva and placed it gently on the man's eyes. "Go and wash in that pool," said Jesus. So, the man went and washed his eyes. He found, to his joy, that he could see for the first time ever!

SEPTEMBER 24

JESUS FOUND MANY WAYS of explaining who he was. One day, he told his followers that he was like a shepherd. "I have come to look after my people, like a shepherd watches over his flock," said Jesus. "But I am not like someone who has been hired to mind the sheep and does not really care about his work. Such a man would run away as soon as he saw a wolf coming. I am a good shepherd. I love my sheep so much that I am prepared to die to keep them safe. I know every one of my sheep, and they all recognize my voice when I call."

September 25

MANY JEWS looked down on people who did not share their faith. They believed that only Jews could go to heaven. "Don't think that being a Jew gives you a ticket to heaven," said Jesus. He told a story. "A man asked his friends to a party. On the day of the party, they all gave excuses why they couldn't come. So, the man called his servant. 'Go into town and invite all the poor, sick, and hungry people to my party,' he said. 'Those I invited first are no longer welcome.' " Jesus was warning the Jews that only people who responded to his teachings would go to heaven.

SEPTEMBER 26

HUGE CROWDS of people followed Jesus everywhere. Many of them wanted to become his disciples. Jesus tried to explain to them what a big step this was. "Have any of you ever built a tower?" he asked. "If so, you must have worked out whether you had enough money to finish the job before you started digging the foundations. Imagine you are a king preparing for battle. Would you send your soldiers off to fight if you weren't absolutely sure they could win? In the same way, you must be sure you have got what it takes to be one of my disciples. You must be willing to give up everything to follow me."

SEPTEMBER 27

ONE DAY, Jesus was talking to a group of tax collectors. Some Jewish teachers were standing nearby. "Look at how Jesus makes friends with sinners," they muttered to each other. Jesus heard what they were saying. "Imagine you owned a hundred sheep," he said to them. "If one of them got lost, wouldn't you leave the rest to go and search for it? And, when you found the missing sheep, would you not have a party to celebrate?" asked Jesus. "In the same way, there is more joy in heaven over one sinner who says sorry to God than over ninety-nine good people who do not need to repent."

SEPTEMBER 28

JESUS THEN TOLD the Jewish teachers another story. "There was a woman who had ten silver coins. One day, she realized that she had lost one of them. The coins were precious to her, and she searched her house from top to bottom for the one that was missing. Suddenly, she saw a glint of silver in a dark corner – it was the lost coin! She was so happy she went to tell all her friends, and they all celebrated the good news." Jesus paused for a moment. "This is what it is like in heaven when a sinner who was lost turns back to God," he explained.

SEPTEMBER 29

"THERE WAS once a man with two sons," said Jesus. "The younger son asked for his share of the family fortune, so his father gave him a large sum of money. Soon afterward, this greedy son left home. He went to live in a foreign country and quickly spent all his father's riches. Then a terrible famine struck. The young man was penniless and starving. 'Why am I so miserable here? Even my father's servants have more to eat than I do,' he thought. 'I shall go back to my father and beg him to forgive me. Perhaps he will take me in to work for him.' "

SEPTEMBER 30

"WHEN THE YOUNG MAN arrived home, his father ran out to greet him. The son began to say sorry for what he had done, but his father would not let him finish. 'Prepare a feast!' he ordered a servant. 'My son was lost, but now he is found!' The older son was jealous of the way his brother had been welcomed. 'I have always obeyed you, father,' he said. 'But you have never made such a fuss of me.' The old man was quick to reassure his older son. 'Everything I have is also yours. But now let's be joyful, because the son I thought was dead is alive again.' "

OCTOBER 1

JESUS' FRIEND LAZARUS

was very ill. Lazarus' sisters, Martha and Mary, were frantic with worry. They sent a message to Jesus, asking him to come at once to make Lazarus well again. Jesus got their message, but he did not leave right away. He stayed where he was, teaching and healing people. Two days later, Jesus set off for Lazarus' home in Bethany. "My friend has fallen asleep, and I must go and wake him up," Jesus told his disciples. They did not understand what Jesus was saying. "Lazarus is already dead," said Jesus. "When you see what I am about to do, you will believe in me."

284

OCTOBER 2

WHEN JESUS ARRIVED in Bethany, Lazarus had already been in his tomb for four days. Martha ran to meet him. "If only you had got here sooner, you could have saved my brother!" she cried. Jesus comforted her. "I am the Resurrection and the Life," he said. "People who believe in me will live again, even if they have died." Then Mary came out of the house. When Jesus saw how grief-stricken she was, it moved him to tears. They went to Lazarus' tomb. "Roll back the stone!" ordered Jesus. There was a gasp as Lazarus walked out into the sunlight. Friends unwrapped the funeral cloths from Lazarus' body, and he returned home with his sisters.

OCTOBER 3

JESUS WAS ON HIS WAY to Jerusalem when he stopped at a village. Ten men called out to him for help. They were all suffering from a terrible skin disease called leprosy. "Go to your local priest and show him that you have been healed," Jesus told the men. As they went off to see the priest, they all became well again.

Out of the whole group, only one man returned to thank Jesus. He was from the nearby country of Samaria. "Where are the other nine men?" asked Jesus. "This man alone has remembered to give praise to God for healing him, and he comes from a foreign land."

OCTOBER 4

JESUS KNEW that some people thought they were better than everyone else. Jesus told these people a story to make them understand how important it was not to look down on others. "Two men went to the temple. One was a Jewish teacher, and the other was a tax collector. The teacher stood up. 'Thank you, God, that I am not sinful,' he prayed in a loud voice. 'I obey your laws and give lots of money to the poor.' The tax collector bowed his head in shame. 'Forgive me, God, for I have sinned,' he whispered. It was the humble tax collector, not the proud teacher, who found favor in the eyes of God."

287

OCTOBER 5

MANY PEOPLE BROUGHT their babies and children to Jesus for a special blessing. When the disciples saw what was happening, they told the parents not to bother Jesus. But Jesus did not want parents to stop bringing their children to him. "Let the children come to me, and do not try to stop them," he told his disciples. "Believe me when I say that heaven belongs to little ones like them. Anyone who does not accept God's word with the love and trust of a child will never enter the Kingdom of Heaven."

OCTOBER 6

A RICH MAN came to see Jesus. "What must I do to have eternal life in the Kingdom of Heaven?" he asked. "I have kept all God's laws since I was a boy." Jesus could see that the man loved one thing more than God, and this was his great wealth. "Give all your money to the poor, so you will have treasure in heaven.

Then follow me." The rich man left with a sad heart, because he knew he could not do this. "It is hard for a rich person to enter God's kingdom," Jesus told his disciples. "In fact, it would be easier for a camel to go through the eye of a needle!"

OCTOBER 7

A BLIND MAN was begging by the road just outside Jericho, when he heard the sound of excited cheers. He asked someone what was going on. "Jesus is passing this way," came the reply. The blind beggar called out in a loud voice, "Lord, have mercy on me!" Some people told him to be quiet, but this only made him shout louder. Jesus stopped. "What is the matter?" he asked. "I want to see!" cried the beggar. "Then open your eyes," said Jesus. "Your faith has healed you."

OCTOBER 8

WHEN JESUS ENTERED

Jericho, large crowds were waiting. A tax collector named Zacchaeus was desperate to see Jesus. But Zacchaeus was not very tall, so he climbed a tree to get a better view. Jesus stopped under the tree. "Come down," said Jesus. "I want to eat at your house." Some of the people were angry. "Why would Jesus go to a sinner's house?" they asked. But from then on, Zacchaeus was a changed man. He gave half of all he had to help the poor and paid back those he had cheated four times what he owed them.

OCTOBER 9

JESUS WANTED PEOPLE to understand that God expected everyone to do their best with whatever they have been given. So he told this parable. "A rich man went on a journey," Jesus began. "Before he left, he gave each of his servants ten coins. When he returned, he called for the servants. One stepped forward proudly. 'I put your money to work and your coins are worth double now,' he said. The rich man was very pleased. Another servant spoke up. 'I hid your coins, because I was afraid of losing the money,' he confessed. The master was angry. 'You lazy servant! You have done nothing, so now I will take away what I gave you in the first place.'"

OCTOBER 10

MARY AND HER SISTER MARTHA were especially grateful to Jesus since he brought their brother Lazarus back from the dead. Just before Passover, they invited Jesus to their house for a special meal. While Martha served the food, Mary took some expensive perfume and poured it over Jesus' feet. This made one disciple very angry. "You could have sold that perfume and given the money to the poor," he complained. "Leave her alone," said Jesus. "Poor people will always be there for you to help," he explained. "But I will not be with you for much longer."

OCTOBER 11

AS JESUS APPROACHED Jerusalem for Passover, he sent two disciples ahead of him. "You will find a donkey in the next village. Untie it for me," he told them. As Jesus rode the donkey into the city, crowds of people waved palm branches high in the air and threw their cloaks down before Jesus. "Make way for the king, who comes in the name of the Lord," they sang. So, Jesus fulfilled the prophesy of Zechariah, which said, "Look, your king is coming to you. He is humble, riding on a donkey."

OCTOBER 12

JESUS KNEW that he was going to leave his disciples soon. He also knew that he would come back one day to rule the Kingdom of Heaven on Earth. Only God knew when this would be. People needed to be ready, because it could happen at any time. "When I come back, it will be like this," Jesus said. "Imagine ten bridesmaids waiting for the bridegroom to arrive. Five of them

have brought enough oil to keep their lamps alight all night, so that they can escort the bridegroom to the wedding. The other five are not well prepared, and their lamps go out halfway through the evening. While they are off buying more oil, the bridegroom arrives, and those five foolish girls miss the wedding celebrations."

OCTOBER 13

WHEN JESUS ARRIVED in Jerusalem, he went to the temple. He had visited this holy place since he was a child. As Jesus entered the courtyards around the temple, he was shocked to see that there were market stalls everywhere. Honest people who had come to the temple to worship God were being cheated out of their money by traders selling goods at high prices. Jesus was furious and drove the traders out of the temple grounds. "Get out!" said Jesus. "God's house is a place of prayer, and you have made it into a robbers' den."

OCTOBER 14

JESUS TOLD this parable. "A man rented a vineyard to some farmers," he said. "At harvest time, he sent a servant for some of the grapes. But the farmers attacked the servant and refused to give him anything. The man sent two more servants, but they were also beaten. 'I'll send my son,' thought the man. 'They'll listen to him.' But the farmers murdered the boy. So, his father killed the farmers and gave his vineyard to some other people." In this story, the father is God, his servants are the prophets he sent to warn his people, and the tenants are the Jewish leaders who would not listen to them. The son is Jesus, and he knows that 'the tenants' will kill him.

OCTOBER 15

JESUS TOLD a story to some important Jewish leaders. "A man asked his sons to work in his vineyard for a day. 'I'm too busy,' said one. But later, he went to help. The other son agreed to lend a hand, but he did not keep his word." Jesus paused. "Which son pleased his father?" he asked. "The one who helped him," they replied. "Change your ways before it is too late," Jesus told them. "Sinners who have repented are going to heaven ahead of you." These leaders were like the second son. They promised to do God's work, but then let God down.

OCTOBER 16

THE TIME CAME for Jesus and his disciples to celebrate the festival of Passover. They entered the upstairs room of a house in Jerusalem, where a meal had been prepared for them. As they waited to be served, Jesus did something surprising. He poured water into a bowl, knelt down, and began to wash his disciples' dirty feet. Then he dried them with a towel. "I am your Lord and master, yet you have just seen me wash your feet," said Jesus. "Now you must follow my example. Forget how important you are, and care for each other, just as I have cared for you."

OCTOBER 17

THE TWELVE DISCIPLES SPENT three years with Jesus, learning about God's kingdom. Jesus knew that this time was coming to an end. At the Jewish festival of the Passover, Jesus and the disciples shared a special meal. This was to be the last supper they would eat together. Jesus took some bread and wine. He told his friends that the bread was like his body and the wine like his blood. Jesus was talking about his own death. He was saying that he was going to sacrifice his body and blood to save people from their sins.

OCTOBER 18

AFTER THEIR LAST SUPPER

together, Jesus and his disciples went
to the Mount of Olives. Jesus told
his disciples to pray, then he walked a
short distance away so that he could
talk to God alone. Jesus knew it was
God's plan for him to suffer and die, so he
asked God to help him during the difficult time ahead.
God answered Jesus' prayer, sending an angel to give
him strength. Jesus returned to the place where he had
left his disciples. They had all fallen asleep because they
were so exhausted. "Wake up!" said Jesus.
"You must pray that God will
keep you from temptation."

OCTOBER 19

THE QUIET CALM of the Mount of Olives was suddenly shattered. A group of people approached Jesus. Their blazing torches lit up the dark night. A single figure stepped forward. It was Judas Iscariot, one of Jesus' disciples. He moved toward Jesus to kiss him. This was a sign to the soldiers. They surrounded Jesus, ready to arrest him. The soldiers had come armed with swords and clubs, but Jesus told them to put down their weapons. He went with them peacefully.

OCTOBER 20

THE SOLDIERS took Jesus to the house of the high priest. Peter followed behind at a safe distance. He did not want to be recognized as one of Jesus' disciples. He joined a group of people warming themselves by a fire outside the house. Three people asked Peter if he was a friend of Jesus. Three times he denied it. "I don't even know him!" he protested. Peter was too frightened to admit that he knew Jesus, his friend and teacher.

OCTOBER 21

THE THIRD TIME

that Peter pretended he didn't know Jesus, he heard a cock crowing. It was the dawn of a new, sad day. With horror, Peter suddenly realized what he had done. The night before, during their last supper, Jesus had spoken to Peter. "Three times before the cock crows tomorrow morning, you will deny knowing me." Peter had not wanted to believe him. "No, lord, I would die for you!" But Jesus had been proven right. Peter felt ashamed and very sorry. He went away and wept bitter tears.

OCTOBER 22

JESUS WAS TAKEN before Pontius Pilate, the Roman governor. Pilate did not think that Jesus had committed a crime. To please the crowd, he planned to punish Jesus, then set him free. But the people, egged on by the Jewish leaders, wanted Jesus to die. They asked for Barabbas, a well-known murderer, to be freed instead of Jesus. Pilate gave in to the rabble.

OCTOBER 23

JESUS WAS LED AWAY to a place called "The Skull," just outside Jerusalem. This was where common criminals were put to death. Jesus had been beaten by his guards, so he was too weak to carry his big wooden cross by himself. A man called Simon, from the country of Cyrene, was forced to carry the cross for Jesus. A crowd of people followed behind them. Many women wept with sadness at what was happening. Jesus was nailed to the cross, which was then raised up high for all to see. To his left and right were two men, suffering the same terrible punishment.

OCTOBER 24

JESUS LOOKED DOWN from the cross as Roman soldiers played games. "Father forgive them because they do not know what they are doing," he prayed. The criminals on the crosses on each side of Jesus began to argue. One hurled insults at Jesus, and the other became angry about this. The second turned to Jesus. "Remember me when you go to heaven," he said. Jesus did much more than that. He forgave his sins there and then.

OCTOBER 25

AFTER A WHILE, the sun stopped shining in the sky and darkness fell, even though it was the middle of the day. In Jerusalem, inside God's temple, the holy curtain was ripped in half from top to bottom. Jesus cried out to God, offering up his life to him. Then he died. A Roman soldier, who was standing guard by the crowd, looked up at the cross. He gave thanks to God for Jesus and said, "This was a good and holy man." Many people watching were very sad at what had happened. They went away, weeping in sorrow.

OCTOBER 26

JOSEPH OF ARIMATHEA was a member of the Jewish Council. But unlike other leaders he did not agree with what had happened to Jesus. Joseph was a rich man, and he thought that Jesus should have a decent burial. Bravely, he went to see Pontius Pilate and asked him for Jesus' body. He took the body to a special tomb cut into the rock in a hillside. He wrapped the body in linen cloth and laid it carefully in the tomb. Then he rolled a big stone across the entrance of the tomb.

OCTOBER 27

VERY EARLY on Sunday morning, Mary Magdalene went to visit the place where Jesus was buried. To her amazement, she found that the stone had been rolled away from the entrance to the tomb. She ran to find Peter and John, Jesus' disciples. "They have taken the Lord's body away!" she told them. Peter and John raced to the tomb and discovered that it was just as Mary had said. All that remained in the tomb were the linen cloths that had been used to cover Jesus' body. The two disciples went home, amazed by what they had seen.

OCTOBER 28

MARY MAGDALENE stood outside the tomb weeping. Then she looked inside the tomb and saw two angels. "Why are you crying?" they asked. "Someone has taken my Lord away," sobbed Mary. She turned to see a man standing nearby. Mistaking him for the gardener, she asked the man where she could find the missing body. The man said, "Mary." All at once, Mary realized who he was. "Teacher!" she cried. "Tell my disciples that I am returning to heaven to be with God, my father," said Jesus.

OCTOBER 29

TWO FOLLOWERS

of Jesus were walking back from Jerusalem to the town of Emmaus when a stranger joined them. "Why are you so sad?" he asked. "Haven't you heard what has happened?" they replied. The stranger was Jesus, but the two friends were kept from recognizing him. As they walked along, Jesus explained the scriptures to them. Then they invited him to have supper with them. When Jesus shared bread with them, they suddenly realized who he was. But Jesus disappeared before their eyes. The two men rushed back to Jerusalem to tell the disciples that Jesus was alive!

OCTOBER 30

LATER THAT NIGHT, the disciples met. They were frightened of being found together, so they locked the doors of the room they were in. Suddenly, Jesus appeared with them. "Peace be with you," he said. Then he showed them the wounds on his hands and ankles from the cross. The disciples were amazed and overjoyed to see Jesus again. "I am sending you out into the world, just as God sent me," Jesus told them. Then he breathed on them. "I am giving you the gift of the Holy Spirit. You now have the same special powers as me to do God's work."

OCTOBER 31

THOMAS WAS NOT with the disciples when Jesus appeared to them. He refused to believe that Jesus really was alive again unless he saw him with his own eyes. A week later the disciples met again in the same house, but this time Thomas was with them. Suddenly, Jesus appeared. He turned to Thomas. "Reach out and touch my wounds, Thomas. Now you need doubt no more!" Thomas fell to his knees. Jesus said, "You believe in me because you have seen me. Blessed are those who do not see me, yet still believe."

NOVEMBER 1

ONE NIGHT, Peter, John, and some other disciples went fishing in a boat. When the sun rose the next morning, their nets were still empty. A man was standing on the shore of the lake. He called out to the disciples. "Throw your nets out from the other side of the boat and you will get a good catch," he told them. They did so, and soon their nets were so full of fish they could hardly drag them back to the boat. Suddenly, John realized who the stranger was. "It's the Lord!" he said to Peter. Right away, Peter jumped into the water and waded toward Jesus.

315

NOVEMBER 2

THE OTHER DISCIPLES followed Peter back to the shore in their boat. They found that Jesus was cooking fish on a fire. "Come and eat breakfast with me," said Jesus. When they had finished, Jesus turned to Peter. "Do you love me?" he asked. "Yes Lord," said Peter, "you know that I do." Then Jesus said, "Feed my lambs." Jesus meant that he wanted Peter to look after his followers. Jesus knew that he would soon be returning to heaven, and his disciples would have to carry on his work alone. Jesus was choosing Peter to be the leader of the disciples. Peter would be the head of the new church that the disciples would build in Jesus' name.

NOVEMBER 3

JESUS APPEARED to his friends many times to show them he was alive again. He wanted to prepare them for their new life without him. He said that they would soon be baptized with the Holy Spirit so that they could begin to do God's work. Soon the time came for Jesus to go back to heaven to be with God. Jesus led his friends to a hill outside Jerusalem. He told his disciples that they must take his teachings to the four corners of the Earth. And then Jesus began to rise up toward heaven.

NOVEMBER 4

THE DISCIPLES STARED up at Jesus as he rose in the sky. They knew that they were seeing him for the last time. Suddenly, a bright cloud hid him from their sight. Then, from nowhere, two men appeared and stood beside the disciples. They were dressed in dazzling white. "One day, Jesus will return to Earth in the same way that you have just seen him go," said the men. Then the disciples walked back to Jerusalem, amazed by what they had seen and heard. When they arrived, they were joined by other followers of Jesus.

NOVEMBER 5

THE DISCIPLES stayed in Jerusalem, as Jesus had said, waiting to be baptized by the Holy Spirit. During this time they chose another disciple to replace Judas Iscariot, who had betrayed Jesus. One morning, the disciples were all together when

they heard a great whooshing noise, like a strong wind. A small flame came to rest on each disciple's head, and they were filled with the power of the Holy Spirit. They rushed outside to tell people what had happened. Amazingly, they found that they could speak in many languages, so that everyone could understand them. The disciples realized that this was the baptism that Jesus had spoken about.

November 6

SOME PEOPLE in the crowd began to whisper to each other, "These men are just drunk." But Peter stood up to explain. "We have been filled with God's Holy Spirit. Do you remember Jesus, who you put to death? It was God's plan that he should die, so we can all be forgiven for our sins. Now Jesus is alive again!" The people were shocked by Peter's words. "What can we do?" they asked. "Tell God you are sorry for your sins, and put your trust in Jesus," replied Peter. "Then the Holy Spirit will come to you, too."

NOVEMBER 7

THE DAY that the Holy Spirit first came to the disciples is called Pentecost. When people began to follow Jesus after Pentecost, some were confused about the Holy Spirit and the gifts it gave to people. They found it difficult to understand why different people received such

different gifts. "Are some gifts better than others? they asked. A follower of Jesus named Paul tried to explain the gifts of the Spirit. He wrote about them in a letter. "People have a variety of gifts, but the same Holy Spirit gives them all," wrote Paul. "Some believers receive the gift of wisdom, while others receive the gift of knowledge. Some are given strong faith, and others are given the ability to heal the sick. Some gifts seem more extraordinary than others, but they are all equally important to God. The gifts of the Holy Spirit are given to be used for the good of everyone."

NOVEMBER 8

THE DISCIPLES PERSUADED many people to change their lives and follow Jesus. On the first day that Peter preached to the crowds, the number of believers increased to three thousand. All the new believers were eager to find out more about Jesus. They spent much of their time learning from Peter and the other disciples. The believers met together to pray and find friendship. They ate meals with each other and shared their things. They sold all their possessions and gave the money to people in their group who needed help. As the days passed, the number of believers grew and grew.

NOVEMBER 9

PETER AND JOHN were going to the temple to pray when they met a beggar. The man had never been able to walk and spent every day lying beside a temple gateway, asking passersby for money. Peter looked straight at the man. "I do not have any coins to give you," he said. "But I can give you what I do have. In the name of Jesus Christ, get up and walk!" Peter reached out to the man and helped him to his feet. The man tried a few steps, then he began to run and jump. He rushed into the temple to give thanks to God.

NOVEMBER 10

WHEN PETER HEALED the lame man, the people watching thought Peter had special powers of his own. But Peter told them that his powers came from Jesus. "Jesus Christ, who died not long ago, is alive again!" said Peter. "Jesus has made this man walk." Peter and John persuaded more and more people to believe in Jesus. The Jewish leaders did not like Peter and John saying that Jesus was alive, so they arrested them.

But nobody could decide how to punish the two men, so they let them go.

November 11

As soon as they were released, Peter and John went straight to their friends. They told them how the Jewish leaders had tried to stop them from spreading the good news about Jesus. The friends, who became known as Christians, gathered together to pray. First they gave thanks for God's greatness. Then they prayed for courage to keep preaching about Jesus. They finished by asking God to allow them to perform more miracles in the name of Jesus, to show the crowds his amazing power. God listened to the disciples' prayers. The Holy Spirit gave them fresh courage and helped them to speak out to the people.

NOVEMBER 12

JESUS' DISCIPLES were busy looking after the many new followers and making sure everyone had enough food to eat. They wanted more time to tell people about Jesus, so they put seven men in charge of sharing the food. Stephen was one of the seven who gave out food. He was also wise and full of faith. He performed many miracles, and those he spoke to soon believed that Jesus was the Savior they had been waiting for. But a group of Jews wanted to stop Stephen from talking about Jesus. So they made up a list of things they said he had done wrong. Then they took him to a court of Jewish leaders.

NOVEMBER 13

THE ANGRY LEADERS

listened to all the bad things that Stephen's accusers said he had done. But, even they noticed that his face was like the face of an angel, shining with light. Soon it was Stephen's turn to talk. He knew he had done nothing wrong. Stephen told how the Jewish people had often turned away from God's chosen leaders. "And now," he said, "you have killed the most important one of all – Jesus, the Son of God!" The Jewish leaders were angrier than ever when they heard these words. They dragged Stephen outside the city, where they threw rocks at him. Stephen knew he was going to die and be with Jesus. He asked God to forgive his enemies.

327

NOVEMBER 14

A MAN NAMED PAUL was one of those who watched Stephen die. Paul did not believe in Jesus, and he was happy to see Stephen stoned to death. The number of Jesus' followers in Jerusalem was growing, and this made Paul very angry. On the day that Stephen was killed, Paul led a big hunt for Jesus' followers. He went all over the city looking for believers. When he found them, he dragged them from their houses and put them in jail. The followers of Jesus were so afraid that they all left Jerusalem. Only Jesus' disciples stayed.

NOVEMBER 15

LIKE STEPHEN, Philip had been one of the seven helpers. When Philip fled Jerusalem, he went to live in the city of Samaria, where he taught about Jesus and performed many miracles. A magician named Simon was envious of Philip's powers. Soon Peter and John came to visit Philip. When Simon saw the disciples baptizing people, he wanted to buy this gift. "Pray to God to forgive you," said Peter. "You can't buy the Holy Spirit!"

NOVEMBER 16

ONE DAY, God told Philip to leave Samaria and take a lonely road through the middle of the desert. As Philip was walking along, he met a man from Ethiopia. This man was an important minister in the queen of Ethiopia's court. He was sitting in his chariot, reading from the words of the prophet Isaiah. There was a puzzled expression on his face. "Do you understand what you are reading?" Philip asked the man. "How can I, when I have no one to tell me what the scriptures mean?" he replied. "Please sit by me and explain them if you can."

NOVEMBER 17

PHILIP CLIMBED into the chariot and began to explain to the man the passage he was reading. "Hundreds of years ago, the prophet Isaiah was looking ahead to the life and death of Jesus," said Philip. "When Isaiah wrote about a servant of God who would be killed like an innocent lamb, he was really telling us about Jesus. Now, our sins can be forgiven because Jesus died for us on the cross." As they were riding along in the chariot, they came to a pool of water. "Stop!" ordered the man. He turned to Philip. "Baptize me, for I know Jesus came to save me," he said. So Philip baptized him there and then.

NOVEMBER 18

PAUL DID NOT BELIEVE in Jesus. He wanted to punish anyone who said that Jesus was God's promised Messiah. One day, Paul was traveling from Jerusalem to the city of Damascus. Suddenly, a dazzling light filled the sky. A loud voice spoke from heaven, saying, "Paul! Why are you being so cruel to me?" Paul fell to his knees. "Who are you, Lord?" he cried. "I am Jesus," came the reply. "Go on to Damascus and I will tell you what you must do." When Paul got up, he found that he could not see. His friends had to lead him by the hand.

November 19

WHEN PAUL REACHED Damascus, he was taken to a friend's house. For three days, he did not eat or drink. Jesus told Ananias, one of his followers, to go to see Paul. At first, Ananias was afraid. He had heard how much Paul hated Jesus' followers. But Jesus told Ananias not to worry. "I have chosen Paul to go out into the world and tell everyone about me," said Jesus. So Ananias went to find Paul. He put his hands over Paul's eyes and healed him. Then he baptized Paul. Paul was now ready to begin his work for Jesus.

NOVEMBER 20

PAUL BEGAN PREACHING

to the people of Damascus. "Jesus is the son of God!" he told the crowds. The people were astonished. "Isn't this the same man who hated Jesus and his followers?" they asked. Some people were happy to see that Paul had changed his ways, but others now regarded him as an enemy and plotted to kill him. They watched the city gates, hoping to capture Paul as he left Damascus. But Paul's new friends heard about the plot and helped him to escape. In the middle of the night, they hid him in a basket. Then they lowered the basket through a hole in the city wall. Paul returned safely to Jerusalem.

November 21

WHEN PAUL ARRIVED in Jerusalem, he wanted to join the disciples. But they were scared of him. "He is just tricking us," they said. "Paul does not really believe in Jesus." There was one disciple, named Barnabas, who did trust Paul. He told his friends how Paul had met Jesus on the road to Damascus. The disciples listened to Barnabas and agreed to let Paul help them with their work. Paul and Barnabas became good friends. God chose them to go on a special journey together to teach more people about Jesus. They sailed away in a boat to the island of Cyprus.

335

NOVEMBER 22

PETER SPENT much of his time preaching to crowds in the towns and villages near Jerusalem. Many people believed Peter's words and became followers of Jesus. One day, Peter stopped in a place called Lydda. He wanted to visit some new believers to give them help and encouragement. He met a man named Aeneas who could not walk. He had not been out of his bed for eight years! "Aeneas," said Peter firmly. "Get up at once! Jesus Christ has healed you!" Aeneas leapt to his feet and shouted for joy. Everyone who saw what had happened followed Jesus from that day on.

NOVEMBER 23

WHILE PETER was in Lydda, two men came up to him with an urgent request. "Come with us to Joppa, a seaside town not far from here," they said. "A faithful disciple of Jesus named Dorcas has just died. She was a good woman, and her friends are very sad." Peter went to Dorcas' house and was met by a group of weeping women. He asked them all to leave the room where Dorcas lay. Peter knelt down and prayed. Then he turned to Dorcas. "Get up!" he said. Dorcas opened her eyes and blinked. When her friends saw that Dorcas was alive, they told everyone they met about Jesus.

337

NOVEMBER 24

PETER STAYED IN JOPPA for a while. One day, he went up to pray on the flat roof of his house. The warm sun made him drowsy, and he fell asleep. He dreamed of a large sheet being lowered to the ground. Inside the sheet were all kinds of creatures that the Jews were forbidden to eat. God told Peter to kill and eat one of the creatures. "Nothing here is unfit for you to eat, because I say that it is clean." Peter woke up and wondered what his strange dream meant.

NOVEMBER 25

PETER WAS STILL WONDERING about his strange dream when he heard some people knocking on his door. God told Peter to welcome the visitors. "I have sent them to you," he said. Peter's visitors worked for a Roman centurion named Cornelius. Cornelius had seen an angel in a vision. "Send some men to Joppa to find a man called Peter," the angel had said. "He will teach you about God." When Peter met Cornelius, he began to understand his dream. Cornelius was not a Jew, but God still wanted him to learn about Jesus. This was because no one was "unclean" in God's sight. Jesus had come to save everyone, not just the Jews.

NOVEMBER 26

KING HEROD AGRIPPA

made life difficult and dangerous for the believers in Jerusalem. He arrested James, one of Jesus' original twelve disciples, and put him to death. Then Herod threw Peter into prison, intending to have him tried and killed after the festival of Passover. Peter was guarded day and night by a squad of soldiers. The night before Peter's trial, an angel appeared in his cell. Peter was asleep. "Get up!" ordered the angel. At once, the chains fell away from Peter's wrists and ankles. "Now come with me," said the angel.

NOVEMBER 27

IN A DAZE, Peter followed the angel through the prison gates and out into the streets of Jerusalem. Then the angel left as suddenly as he had appeared. Peter realized that he was not dreaming. He was a free man again! He went to the house of one of his friends and knocked on the door. A servant girl named Rhoda answered and rushed to tell everyone in the house that Peter had come. But no one would believe her until they went to the door and saw Peter for themselves. Peter went inside and told his friends about his amazing escape.

November 28

PAUL AND BARNABAS traveled around Cyprus, preaching to the people. The Roman ruler of the island, Sergius Paulus, heard about the two men. He wanted to hear what they had to say, so he sent for them. Elymas was one of Sergius' servants. He tried to stop his master from listening to Paul and Barnabas. Paul became angry with Elymas. "It is time to stop your wickedness," he said. "God is going to punish you. For a time, you will not be able to see the light of the sun." Sergius watched as Elymas stumbled and fell. His servant had gone blind. Amazed at what he had seen and heard, Sergius began to believe in Jesus.

NOVEMBER 29

AFTER A TIME, Paul and Barnabas left Cyprus and sailed to a country that is now called Turkey. They went from town to town preaching the good news about Jesus. In the town of Lystra, people had not even heard of God. They worshipped many different gods. When Paul healed a lame man there, the people thought that the two men were gods in human form. They brought bulls wreathed with flowers to sacrifice to them. "Stop!" cried Paul. "We are just ordinary people like you. We have come to tell you about the one true God and his son, Jesus Christ." At this, the people began to listen.

NOVEMBER 30

FOR SEVERAL YEARS,
Paul and Barnabas traveled from place to place, telling everyone about Jesus. Sometimes people were hostile. Once, Paul was stoned by an angry crowd. But Paul and Barnabas never gave up. Many people began to follow Jesus, and new churches sprang up all over. Paul and Barnabas appointed elders in all the churches to look after the new followers of Jesus. After a time, they began to worry about the Christians they had left behind, and they decided to go back to visit them. Paul and Barnabas argued over whom to take with them. In the end, they set off in different directions, each with a new companion. Barnabas chose Mark and sailed to Cyprus. Paul chose Silas and traveled through Syria and Cilicia.

DECEMBER 1

PAUL AND SILAS visited many churches to encourage the new Christians. Paul retraced his steps and returned to Lystra. It was here, just a few years before, that the people had wanted to worship Paul and Barnabas as gods. But many had listened to their teachings and had become followers of Jesus. One of these new Christians was a young man named Timothy. Paul was impressed by the strength of Timothy's faith, and so he invited Timothy to join them in their work. The three men traveled together, helping the churches and preaching about Jesus.

DECEMBER 2

PAUL, SILAS, and Timothy did not decide for themselves which route to take; they went wherever the Holy Spirit told them to go. Sometimes they arrived at a place, but did not enter it because the Holy Spirit told them to pass it by. They traveled by land and sea, and everywhere they went they taught people about Jesus. When the three men reached Troas, near the ancient city of Troy, Paul had a strange dream. A man was pleading with him, saying, "Please come and help us in Macedonia." Paul realized at once that God was calling him to go to that country to preach to the people there about Jesus. So, Paul, Silas, and Timothy got on a boat to Macedonia.

DECEMBER 3

WHEN PAUL, SILAS, and Timothy reached Macedonia, they traveled on to Philippi, an ancient city in what is now northeastern Greece. On the Sabbath, the three friends went outside the city gates, looking for a quiet place to pray. Here they met some women sitting by a river. Paul began to talk to them about Jesus. One, a wealthy businesswoman named Lydia, became a believer. Paul baptized her in the river, along with her family and servants. Lydia invited Paul and his friends to stay at her house, and they accepted.

DECEMBER 4

ONE DAY, Paul and Silas were going to the river outside Philippi to pray, when they met a slave girl who could tell people's fortunes. The girl was filled with an evil spirit, so Paul ordered the spirit to leave her. When the slave girl's owners realized that she could no longer earn money for them, they were furious. They had Paul and Silas beaten and then thrown into prison. That night, Paul and Silas sang praises to God in their prison cell. The other prisoners listened quietly. Suddenly, the prison was shaken by a violent earthquake. The prisoners' chains broke away from the walls, and the doors swung open.

DECEMBER 5

THE PRISON GUARD was terrified. He thought all his prisoners had escaped and that he was in big trouble. He pulled out a sword to kill himself, but Paul shouted, "Don't hurt yourself, we're still here!" The guard fell to his knees. "How can I be saved?" he asked. Paul told him about Jesus, and the man became a believer. He took Paul and Silas back to his home. Soon, the guard's family decided to follow Jesus, too. The next day, city officials came to say sorry to Paul and Silas for the way they had been treated. Then Paul and Silas were set free.

DECEMBER 6

PAUL AND HIS FRIENDS left Philippi and traveled to the city of Thessalonica. Paul visited the synagogue, where the Jews went to pray. He told the people there all about Jesus. Paul's teachings persuaded many of the Jews to follow Jesus. But there were some Jews who were jealous of Paul's popularity. They started a riot and tried to put the blame on Paul and his companions. They looked everywhere for the three men, but they could not find them. So they rounded up some of the new believers and got them into trouble with the city leaders by saying that they worshipped a new king named Jesus.

DECEMBER 7

PAUL NEVER STAYED in one place for long, because he knew God wanted him to spread the good news about Jesus. But Paul never forgot the believers that he left behind. He often wondered how the new churches were getting along, and he tried to keep in touch with them by writing letters. Some time after Paul left Thessalonica, he wrote two letters to the new Christians to give advice and encouragement.

In these letters, Paul told them to live good and holy lives, and to be ready for the day when Jesus would return to Earth.

December 8

The NEXT STOP on their travels was the town of Berea. As soon as Paul and his companions began to preach there, they found that the people were eager to listen. Both Jews and Greeks became believers. News of this soon got back to Thessalonica. The Jews who had stirred up riots in Thessalonica went to Berea to turn the crowds against Paul and his friends. Paul did not want to be thrown into prison, because this would stop him spreading the news about Jesus. So he left Berea and headed for the coast. Silas and Timothy promised to follow Paul as soon as they could.

DECEMBER 9

PAUL WAITED for Silas and Timothy in Athens. He was sad to see how many statues of different gods there were all over the city. The people of Athens loved to discuss ideas and were happy to argue with Paul. One day, Paul stood up at a meeting to explain his faith. "God is far greater than anything that can be made by human hands," said Paul. "God created this world and everything in it." When he told the group that Jesus had been raised from the dead to save them from their sins, some of the people sneered and did not believe Paul. But others listened carefully and believed Paul's message.

DECEMBER 10

PAUL LEFT ATHENS and moved to Corinth, where he was joined by Silas and Timothy. As usual, Paul taught first in the synagogue. But some of the Jews there began to insult him. "I wash my hands of you!" Paul told them angrily. "From now on I'll teach the non-Jews first." The Jews accused Paul of breaking the law and dragged him before Gallio, the Roman ruler of Corinth. God told Paul not to be afraid. "I will take care of you," said God. Gallio said that Paul had done nothing wrong under Roman law and threw his accusers out of court.

DECEMBER 11

WHILE IN CORINTH, Paul stayed at the home of Priscilla and Aquila. They had been thrown out of Rome because they were Jews. When Priscilla and Aquila met Paul, they became Christians.

The three became good friends.
When Paul decided to leave Corinth,
Priscilla and Aquila went with him. They sailed to Ephesus, where Paul spoke in the synagogue. The Jews there were very interested in what Paul had to say about Jesus. Priscilla and Aquila stayed on in Ephesus after Paul had left. They had learned a lot about Jesus, so they were able to teach the people, and they won many new believers.

December 12

PAUL LEFT EPHESUS to spread the news about Jesus in other places. Soon afterward, a Jew named Apollos arrived in Ephesus. Apollos was a very smart man and knew the scriptures inside out. He had heard all about Jesus from the teachings of John the Baptist, and he began to tell people about him. Priscilla and Aquila heard Apollos speaking in the synagogue. They invited Apollos into their home and told him everything that Paul had taught them about Jesus. Apollos then used his great intelligence and understanding to prove to people that Jesus really was God's promised Savior. With Apollos' help, the number of Christians in Ephesus grew and grew.

December 13

PAUL RETURNED to Ephesus and stayed there for three years. The city was famous for its temple to Artemis, a Greek goddess. Many people were worshippers of Artemis, and there was a good trade in silver models of the goddess. But Paul had won over so many people to Christianity that the local silversmiths were getting worried. They decided to march through the city, shouting praise to Artemis. Many passersby joined in, and the march turned into a riot. Paul wanted to speak to the rioters, but it was too dangerous. Eventually, a town clerk calmed the angry crowds by telling them that Paul had meant the people of Ephesus no harm.

357

DECEMBER 14

NOT LONG AFTER the trouble in Ephesus, Paul left the city. He stopped for a short time in the town of Troas. The believers there crowded together in an upstairs room to listen to Paul. It was evening, and as midnight approached some of the group felt sleepy. A man named Eutychus was sitting on a window sill. He dozed off and fell backward out of the open window onto the ground below. Everybody rushed outside, but it was too late. Eutychus was dead. Paul took him in his arms. "Don't worry, he's alive!" he cried. Sure enough, Eutychus staggered to his feet, and everyone praised God for the miracle.

DECEMBER 15

PAUL WANTED TO REACH Jerusalem in time for Pentecost to celebrate the arrival of the Holy Spirit with the Christians there. He left Troas the day after Eutychus' accident. Paul felt he hadn't said a real goodbye to his friends in Ephesus. So, on his way back to Jerusalem, he broke his journey and sent a message to the church leaders there to come and see him.

The church leaders came at once. Paul spoke to them about his past work and his hopes and fears for the future. "You will never see me again," he said sadly. "Take care of God's church in Ephesus." They prayed together, then they parted for the last time.

DECEMBER 16

PAUL BROKE HIS JOURNEY to visit Philip, who had been a follower of Jesus even longer than Paul. During Paul's visit, a prophet named Agabus arrived. Agabus took Paul's belt and tied it around his own hands and feet. "If you go to Jerusalem, this is what will happen to you," Agabus told Paul. "You will be captured by Jews and handed over to the Romans." Paul's friends begged him not to go back to the city, but Paul's mind was made up. "I am prepared to die for Jesus," he said. With that, he set off again. Whatever danger awaited him in Jerusalem, he was ready to face it.

DECEMBER 17

WHEN PAUL ARRIVED

in Jerusalem, he went to the temple. Some of his enemies recognized him. "This man is teaching people to break God's laws!" they cried. Soon, the whole city was in uproar. Paul was dragged out of the temple and beaten by the mob. Meanwhile, news reached the commander of the Roman army about the riot. He rushed to the temple with a group of his officers. As soon as the mob saw the soldiers, they stopped beating Paul. "What has this man done?"asked the Roman commander. But the commander could not get to the truth because of the uproar. So he arrested Paul and took him to a nearby fort.

DECEMBER 18

AS THE SOLDIERS took Paul into the fort, Paul turned to look at the angry mob that had followed him. He asked permission from the commander to speak to the crowd. The army chief didn't know who Paul was or where he came from, but he agreed to let his prisoner address the people.

Silence fell as Paul explained how he had once hated the Christians as much as anyone. He told them what had happened to him on the road to Damascus and how he had come to believe in Jesus. He said that God wanted him to preach to everyone, not just the Jews. At this, the people got angry again. "Kill him!" they cried.

DECEMBER 19

THE ARMY COMMANDER was angry with Paul for stirring up the crowds again. "Take this man to be whipped," he ordered his guards. "Then find out what he has done to upset the Jews." As the guards were tying up their prisoner, Paul began to protest. "Isn't it against the law to whip a Roman citizen who has yet to be found guilty of any crime?" he asked. This threw the guards into a panic, and they sent for their leader. "Are you really a Roman citizen?" asked the commander. "Yes, I am," replied Paul. The commander knew that he had to treat a Roman citizen with respect. So, he made sure that no one laid a finger on Paul.

DECEMBER 20

THE NEXT DAY, the army commander brought Paul before a gathering of the Jewish leaders. He wanted to find out what his prisoner had done wrong. Paul spoke to the group, saying, "I am on trial because I believe that the dead can rise again to eternal life." The priests began to argue about what Paul had said. Some of them held the same belief. "We don't think this man is guilty of anything," they said. The argument got so heated that the commander thought Paul would get hurt. So, the guards stepped in and took him back into the fort. The next day, a group of Jews hatched a plot to kill Paul. They made a solemn vow not to eat or drink until Paul was dead.

DECEMBER 21

PAUL'S NEPHEW heard about the plot and rushed to tell his uncle. Paul called the soldier on guard. "Take my nephew to see your commanding officer," he said. The young man told the commander what the Jews had planned. "When the Jewish leaders say they want to see Paul again, do not agree to their request," he said. "They are waiting outside right now, ready to kill my uncle in an ambush." The commander took the warning seriously. He ordered his men to escort Paul out of Jerusalem during the cover of darkness and take him to a place of safety.

DECEMBER 22

THE ARMY COMMANDER sent Paul to nearby Caesarea to stand trial before Felix, the Roman governor. The chief priests came to argue their case against Paul. They accused Paul of stirring up riots among Jews all over the world. But they could give Felix no proof. Paul spoke up to defend himself. "I have done nothing wrong!" he cried. Felix could not make up his mind what to do. He didn't want to upset the Jews, so he kept Paul in prison. Two years later, a new governor named Festus took over from Felix. Festus tried to persuade Paul to return to Jerusalem to face a Jewish court, but Paul knew that the Jews would kill him. "I demand to be tried in Rome, because I am a Roman citizen!" said Paul.

DECEMBER 23

A FEW DAYS LATER, King Agrippa visited Festus. The governor shared his problem with the king. "I have a prisoner who has made some of your Jewish leaders so angry that they want him to be put to death," he said. "As a Roman, I do not believe this man has broken the law." The next day, Paul was brought before King Agrippa. Paul told the king how he had become a Christian, and how he spent all his time persuading others to follow Jesus. Agrippa agreed that Paul did not deserve to die, or even to stay in prison. "If he had not asked to be tried in Rome, you could have set him free," said Agrippa.

DECEMBER 24

FESTUS SENT PAUL to stand trial in Rome. So Paul boarded a ship with some other prisoners. They were guarded by a group of soldiers, under the command of a Roman centurion named Julius. The journey was difficult from the start, with strong winds blowing the ship off course. When the weather got even worse, Paul suggested that they stop in a port for the winter. But his advice was ignored, and the ship sailed straight into a terrible storm. Huge waves battered the ship, and the ship's crew threw all the cargo overboard. For fourteen days, no one ate a thing, because they were all in fear for their lives.

DECEMBER 25

THE ONLY PERSON who was not terrified was Paul. "You should have listened to me!" he said. "But I know that we will all survive. Last night I dreamt God would lead us to safety." Then Paul persuaded everyone to share some food together. "You will need your strength," he said. The next day, the ship ran aground on a sandbank and split apart. The soldiers wanted to kill the prisoners to prevent them from escaping. But Julius stopped the soldiers. All those on board managed to grab pieces of the broken ship and paddle safely to the shore.

DECEMBER 26

THE SURVIVORS of the shipwreck had arrived on the island of Malta. The local people were kind to them and made a bonfire to warm the bedraggled group. As Paul was putting wood on the fire, a poisonous snake slid out of the wood pile and coiled itself around his hand. "This man must be a murderer," said the islanders to one another. "He may have escaped the storm, but justice will not allow him to live!" Paul shook off the snake into the fire. When the islanders saw that Paul was unharmed by the snake, they changed their minds about him and thought he must be a god.

DECEMBER 27

THE ROMAN GOVERNOR

of Malta was named Publius. He welcomed the island's new arrivals and invited them to stay at his luxurious villa. One day, Publius' father fell ill with a fever. Paul said prayers for the old man, then he healed him. News of Paul's amazing powers spread quickly. Soon, those on the island who were sick started coming to Paul to be made well again. Paul and the other shipwrecked victims remained on Malta for three months. When the winter had passed, they set off again on a ship bound for Italy. The people of Malta gave them everything they needed for their journey.

371

December 28

The sea voyage

ended in Puteoli, a port in southern Italy. But, Paul's exhausting journey was not over yet. There were still many miles to travel by road to reach Rome. As Paul approached the city, he was delighted to find that a group of believers were waiting to welcome him and keep him company on the last stretch of his journey. When Paul arrived in Rome, he was treated well. He was not thrown into prison like a common criminal. He was allowed to live in a private house, guarded by a single Roman soldier. He could also have as many visitors as he wished. So, Paul was able to carry on preaching about Jesus.

DECEMBER 29

SOON AFTER HE ARRIVED, Paul invited the Jewish leaders in Rome to come and see him. He told them how the Jewish leaders in Jerusalem had tried to kill him, but they knew nothing about this. Paul tried to convince them that Jesus was the Savior they had been waiting for. Like the Jews in other cities, most of them did not want to listen. So Paul turned his attention to the non-Jews. He knew that the future of the Christian church rested with them, not the Jews. During his two years in Rome, Paul wrote many letters to inspire new believers and to encourage the growing churches.

DECEMBER 30

AS THE CHRISTIAN CHURCH began to grow, it went through a difficult time. The Roman emperor Nero was a cruel ruler. He treated the Christians harshly, and many were imprisoned and killed. John, one of the original twelve disciples of Jesus, was an old man by this time. Despite his age, he was imprisoned on the island of Patmos. One Sunday morning, the Lord Jesus himself appeared to John. He dazzled John with the bright light of his amazing glory. With a loud voice that sounded like a trumpet, Jesus gave John a special message to encourage the Christians.

DECEMBER 31

AS JESUS SPOKE, John had a glimpse of heaven. John found it difficult to describe in words what he saw, so he wrote down his experience in a beautiful kind of picture language. His colorful images can only hint at the spectacular power and might of God's kingdom.

The message that Jesus gave to John is now called the "Revelation." It offered hope of a fresh beginning and a wonderful future for God's people. "I saw a new Heaven and a new Earth," wrote John. "Now God will live with us, and there will be no more crying or sadness. The glory of God will be with us forever."

PEOPLE OF THE OLD TESTAMENT

AARON
Moses' brother. He acted as spokesman when they went to see the king of Egypt.

ABEL
Second son of Adam and Eve. Abel was killed by his jealous brother Cain.

ABRAHAM
The founder of the people of Israel. He obeyed God's call and was always faithful.

ABRAHAM, SARAH, AND ISAAC

ADAM
The first man God created and husband of Eve. The pair sinned against God and had to leave the Garden of Eden.

CAIN
First son of Adam and Eve. He killed his brother Abel in a jealous rage.

DANIEL
An Israelite who rose to an important position in Babylon. He had a gift for interpreting dreams. He was thrown into the lions' den by King Darius.

DAVID
A shepherd boy from Bethlehem. He was chosen by God to become king of Israel. He was also a great musician.

ELIJAH
A great prophet of Israel. He stood up to King Ahab, a bad king who wanted God's people to worship false gods.

ELISHA
The man who followed Elijah as God's prophet.

ESAU
Jacob's twin brother and the son of Isaac and Rebecca.

ESTHER
The young queen of King Xerxes. She saved the Jewish people from massacre.

EVE

EVE
The first woman to be created by God. She tempted Adam to sin against God.

EZEKIEL
A prophet during the period of Babylonian exile. He foretold the fall of Jerusalem.

GOLIATH
A Philistine giant soldier who challenged the Israelites. He was killed by David.

HAMAN
Chief minister of King Xerxes. He plotted to massacre the Jews.

HANNAH
Mother of Samuel.

ISAAC
Son of Abraham and Sarah, husband of Rebecca and father of Esau and Jacob.

ISAIAH
A prophet who foretold the coming of the Messiah.

JACOB
Son of Isaac and Rebecca, and younger twin brother of Esau. He stole Esau's inheritance.

JEREMIAH
A prophet in Judah who warned that Jerusalem would be destroyed and God's people forced into exile.

JOB
A farmer who coped with terrible suffering through his faith in God.

JONAH
A disobedient prophet who was swallowed by a big fish.

JONAH

JONATHAN
The son of King Saul. He warned David that his father wanted to kill him.

JOSEPH
Favorite son of Jacob. He was sold into slavery in Egypt, where he rose to a position of power. He saved Egypt and his family from famine.

JOSHUA
A loyal helper of Moses. He became leader of God's people after Moses' death.

MOSES

MOSES
A great leader and prophet, chosen by God to lead his people out of Egypt and take them to the Promised Land.

NAOMI
The mother-in-law of Ruth.

NEHEMIAH
He helped to rebuild the city of Jerusalem when the Jewish people returned from exile in Babylon.

NOAH
God saved him and his family from the great flood by telling them to build an ark.

RACHEL
Daughter of Laban and wife of Jacob.

REBECCA
Wife of Isaac and mother of Jacob and Esau.

RUTH
Daughter-in-law of Naomi and wife of Boaz.

SAMSON
An Israelite with great strength who fought the Philistines. He lost his strength when the Philistines cut off his hair.

SAMUEL
The prophet who anointed the first kings of Israel, Saul and David.

SARAH
Wife of Abraham and mother of Isaac.

SAUL
The first king of Israel. He later disobeyed God.

SOLOMON
He followed his father David as king of Israel. He built the temple in Jerusalem and was famous for his wisdom.

ZEDEKIAH
The last king of Judah. He was taken prisoner when Jerusalem fell to the Babylonians. He died in exile.

PEOPLE OF THE NEW TESTAMENT

ANANIAS
A follower of Jesus in Damascus who cured Paul of his blindness.

ANDREW
Brother of Peter and one of the twelve disciples.

BARNABAS
A Christian who went with Paul on a journey to Cyprus to teach more people about Jesus.

ELIZABETH AND MARY

ELIZABETH
Wife of Zechariah, mother of John the Baptist, and cousin of Mary.

GABRIEL
An angel and important messenger from God. Gabriel told Mary that she would give birth to Jesus.

HEROD AGRIPPA
Grandson of Herod the Great.

HEROD ANTIPAS
Son of Herod the Great. He gave the order for John the Baptist to be beheaded.

HEROD THE GREAT
King of Judah when Jesus was born. He gave an order for all the baby boys in Bethlehem to be killed.

JAMES
One of the twelve disciples. He was John's brother and a close friend of Jesus.

JESUS
The Son of God, who came to Earth and died to save everyone from their sins.

JOHN THE APOSTLE
One of the twelve disciples and brother of James. He was a close friend of Jesus.

JOHN THE BAPTIST
Son of Zechariah and Elizabeth. He was sent by God to prepare people for the coming of the Messiah. He was beheaded by Herod Antipas.

JOSEPH
A carpenter from Nazareth who married Mary, the mother of Jesus.

JOSEPH OF ARIMATHEA
The man who provided a tomb for Jesus' body.

JUDAS ISCARIOT
One of the twelve disciples. He betrayed Jesus.

LAZARUS
A friend of Jesus and brother of Mary and Martha. Jesus raised him from the dead.

MARTHA
Sister of Mary and Lazarus. A good friend of Jesus.

MARY
The mother of Jesus and wife of Joseph the carpenter.

JOSEPH, MARY, AND JESUS

MARY MAGDALENE
A devoted follower of Jesus. She was the first person to see Jesus after he had risen from the dead.

MARY OF BETHANY
Sister of Martha and Lazarus and a good friend of Jesus. She poured perfume over Jesus' feet before his death.

MATTHEW
A tax collector who became one of the twelve disciples.

PAUL
A persecutor of the early Church who was converted on the road to Damascus. He became the Church's first missionary.

PAUL

PETER
Brother of Andrew, he was one of the twelve disciples. He became head of the first Christians in Jerusalem.

PHILIP
1. One of the twelve disciples.
2. One of the seven helpers. He fled from Jerusalem to Samaria where he performed many miracles.

PONTIUS PILATE

PONTIUS PILATE
Roman governor who gave the order for Jesus to be crucified, even though he believed him to be innocent.

SALOME
Daughter of Herodias who asked Herod Antipas for the head of John the Baptist on a plate.

SILAS
A leader of the early Church. He traveled with Paul on some of his missionary journeys.

SIMON
One of the twelve disciples.

SIMON THE MAGICIAN
A man from Samaria who tried to buy the power of the Holy Spirit from Peter and John.

STEPHEN
One of the first leaders of the early Church. He was the first Christian to be killed for his beliefs.

THOMAS
One of the twelve disciples. He doubted that Jesus had risen from the dead until he saw Jesus' wounds for himself.

TIMOTHY
A young man who joined Paul on some of his missionary journeys.

ZECHARIAH
Father of John the Baptist and husband of Elizabeth. He was a priest at the temple in Jerusalem.

ZECHARIAH

379

INDEX

THE LORD'S PRAYER

OUR FATHER who art in heaven, hallowed be thy name.
Thy kingdom come. Thy will be done, on earth as it is in heaven.
Give us this day our daily bread.
And forgive us our trespasses, as we forgive those who
trespass against us.
And lead us not into temptation.
But deliver us from evil. For thine is the kingdom, the power,
and the glory forever and ever.

Amen.